Models for Improving College Teaching:
A Faculty Resource

by Jon E. Travis

ASHE-ERIC Higher Education Report No. 6, 1995

Prepared by

Clearinghouse on Higher Education
The George Washington University

In cooperation with

Association for the Study
of Higher Education

Published by

Graduate School of Education and Human Development
The George Washington University

Jonathan D. Fife, Series Editor

Cite as

Travis, Jon E. 1995. *Models for Improving College Teaching: A Faculty Resource.* ASHE-ERIC Higher Education Report No. 6. Washington, D.C.: The George Washington University, Graduate School of Education and Human Development.

Library of Congress Catalog Card Number 96-78491
ISSN 0884-0040
ISBN 1-878380-70-2

Managing Editor: Lynne J. Scott
Manuscript Editor: Barbara Fishel/Editech
Cover Design by Michael David Brown, Rockville, Maryland

Publication Date: 1997

The ERIC Clearinghouse on Higher Education invites individuals to submit proposals for writing monographs for the *ASHE-ERIC Higher Education Report* series. Proposals must include:
1. A detailed manuscript proposal of not more than five pages.
2. A chapter-by-chapter outline.
3. A 75-word summary to be used by several review committees for the initial screening and rating of each proposal.
4. A vita and a writing sample.

ERIC **Clearinghouse on Higher Education**
Graduate School of Education and Human Development
The George Washington University
One Dupont Circle, Suite 630
Washington, DC 20036-1183

This publication was prepared partially with funding from the Office of Education Research and Improvement, U.S. Department of Education, under contract no. ED RR-93-002008. The opinions expressed in this report do not necessarily reflect the positions or policies of OERI or the Department.

EXECUTIVE SUMMARY

Colleges and universities increasingly are investing attention and energy on issues related to teaching and learning. Institutions may be reacting to public demands for improved student outcomes or criticism of dominant research agendas. Still, because of the service they provide, some institutions of higher education may be focusing more on teaching and learning out of genuine concern and a sense of responsibility to students. Whether the motivation stems from a disturbed populace or a recognized obligation, colleges are making a commitment to improve student learning.

How well institutions respond to this "new" teaching and learning agenda may be a matter of debate, especially if some of the following criteria are considered: tangible rewards for good teaching, public recognition of faculty, resource centers for instructional development, credit for research and publication of teaching issues, and preparation of graduate students for college teaching (Halpern and Associates 1994). However an individual institution approaches such issues, faculty still bear the major responsibility for student learning (Davis 1993). Hence, faculty are expected to inspire an instructional renaissance (Svinicki 1990). As a consequence, faculty may renew their own commitment to lifelong learning and rekindle once again the excitement of discovery.

What Can Faculty Do to Enhance Students' Learning?

As learning becomes more complex, students frequently depend on faculty to assist them with a multitude of obstacles. Yet given the typical preparation college faculty receive for teaching, the tendency to concentrate on presentational methods, like the lecture, can aggravate students' difficulties with learning. Consequently, instructors are encouraged "to stop viewing teaching as 'covering the content' and to start viewing it as 'helping the students learn'" (Svinicki 1990, p. 7). Such a change in process orientation can lead to a focus on understanding how people learn and the variables and variations of learning that are possible, which can be accomplished through the use of resources designed to facilitate learning by transforming college teaching.

What Resources Can Help Faculty Improve Learning?

To help faculty achieve such an instructional transformation, numerous faculty development programs and professionals promote the development of expertise in teaching. Supporting an array of initiatives, such as instructional grants, workshops and discussion groups, classroom observation, and microteaching, faculty development efforts enable instructors to consider adaptations to their teaching (Weimer 1990). In addition, reference and research information, hardware technology and support, and advisory personnel can augment existing resources. Each opportunity is intended to offer faculty insight into the significant accumulation of knowledge about teaching and learning (Menges, Weimer, and Associates 1996).

Among the resources available for faculty is an array of innovative improvement strategies and classroom methods, such as cooperative learning, the case method, test feedback, and videotaping. Some of these strategies have a formal structure, an extensive research base, and applicability to almost any discipline. Such strategies have been described as "teaching improvement models" (Svinicki 1990).

What Additional Resources Might Faculty Need to Promote Learning?

While these resources, strategies, and models can be beneficial for enhancing learning, the hardworking faculty member in higher education, who often is faced with increasing demands to do more and to be more effective, may not be able to review this vast and diffuse assortment of options (Svinicki 1990). Challenged daily to fulfill their institutional requirements and to meet the needs of a diverse group of students, faculty should have a selection of innovative teaching and learning techniques in an easy-to-use format. Although some faculty development programs may support projects to disseminate information on one or two teaching improvement models, the tendency to group such models for discussion and selection, much like a menu, is rare. Hence, a comprehensive and concise compilation of teaching improvement models could provide faculty with a useful resource not previously available.

What Are Some Models Included in This Collection?

The teaching improvement models included in this report were selected on the basis of their relative novelty for faculty, compared to more familiar strategies like writing-across-the-curriculum or simulation. The collection comprises six categories of models: models for assessment and feedback, discussion and sharing, dissemination, clinical development, teaching and learning, and instructional planning. The models include Classroom Assessment, the Great Teachers Seminar, Integration of Teaching and Learning Styles, the Instructional Skills Workshop, Adaptive Control of Thought, Multiple Intelligences and Teaching, Instructional Event Design, and the Five-Step Process for Improving Teaching. These and other models similarly designed to enhance learning offer specific procedures that can be implemented easily, without formal training.

What Are the Teaching Improvement Models Designed to Do?

One purpose of this collection is to encourage faculty to reflect on the learning process and on the influence of their teaching. Each model selected for improving college teaching was originally designed to meet a distinct faculty need, whether feedback from students, the opportunity to share thoughts and strategies with peers, or the collection and dissemination of ideas among faculty. Other models focus on instructional improvement in a secure environment, course and curriculum design, and an understanding of learning theory and various learning styles.

Why Should College Faculty Consider or Implement These Models?

Higher education in the United States has been challenged to improve students' learning experiences. Given sufficient support and resources, college and university faculty have the capability to enhance their students' learning. The models in this collection offer faculty an assortment of resources to use in this endeavor.

CONTENTS

FOREWORD

The call for improving college teaching is being heard loudly and clearly at all institutions of higher education. Students, parents, legislators, and even college presidents question the effectiveness of college teaching. Legislation has been passed to ensure that each faculty member teaches a minimum number of hours. Boards of trustees question tenure out of fear that it is a barrier to accountability in the classroom. Faculty in turn respond that the quality of their teaching is rarely used for annual and promotional evaluations. And they point out that the amount of funds that the average institution uses to support improvement of teaching as a percentage of personnel dollars is minuscule compared to budgets for human resource development in industries of comparable size.

All parties basically agree that two conditions affect college teaching. The first condition, which is fundamental to the problem, is that graduate schools expose their students only minimally to the knowledge and skills related to teaching. The second is that colleges and universities have assumed that faculty can teach or that poor teaching is an individual, not an institutional, problem. In other words, institutions do not treat the assessment and improvement of teaching as a continuous and institutional concern.

To make a measurable impact on the quality of teaching, the following conditions must exist:

- The institution as a whole must recognize that the improvement of college teaching must be addressed as a continuous, institutionwide concern.
- Faculty, administrators, and students need to be involved to identify reliable and valid assessment tools to measure the quality and effectiveness of college teaching.
- Demonstration of the quality of teaching must become a greater part of annual faculty evaluations.
- Institutions must reinforce their rhetoric about improving college teaching by providing individual faculty opportunities to assess and develop their teaching skills—not only sponsoring voluntary faculty development centers, but also regularly providing faculty information about models of college teaching.

This report by Jon E. Travis, assistant professor of higher education and director of the Center for Community College

Education at Texas A&M University–Commerce, reviews 16 teaching models designed to enhance learning that can be implemented without formal training. The models are grouped to facilitate faculty members' use of the collection: assessment/feedback, discussion/sharing, dissemination, clinical development, teaching/learning, and instructional planning.

By making information on improving college teaching available to every faculty member, developing a culture where the discussion of college teaching becomes a regular part of faculty meetings, and making the improvement of college teaching part of individual faculty development plans, colleges and universities will see significant improvement in the quality of teaching on their campuses.

Jonathan D. Fife
Series Editor,
Professor of Higher Education Administration and
Director, ERIC Clearinghouse on Higher Education

ACKNOWLEDGMENTS

To the community of faculty development professionals—especially Billie Hughes, who introduced me to some of the models for improving college teaching—I owe a debt of gratitude. My appreciation is also offered to Jonathan Fife and his staff for their efforts in support of this project. College faculty who consistently seek more and better ways to improve their teaching deserve a special note of thanks. And I wish to recognize my wife, Jacalyn, and my colleagues at Texas A&M University–Commerce for their patience and understanding throughout this project.

INTRODUCTION

Education is a necessity in our modern culture. Yet while attaining an education may be a generally accepted goal of American life, criticism of schools and educators has become common. The professoriat in this country is one of the more recent targets of such attacks. Believing that faculty are committed to establishing themselves as independent contractors who tenaciously defend tenure as a haven from accountability, the critics have suggested that college and university faculty are at fault for a supposed demise of higher education in the United States (Bérubé 1996; Kerschner and Kegley 1994).

Despite any public opinion to the contrary, college and university faculty are dedicated professionals who are genuinely concerned about what takes place in the classroom. If the effectiveness of teaching has diminished in higher education, the faculty have not single-handedly caused such a presumed decline. Based on the typical reward procedures for faculty, most four-year institutions clearly emphasize research and publication over teaching (Cannon 1989; Halpern 1994). Further, college and university faculty often have not been adequately prepared for teaching at the college level (Boice 1992; Eble 1988; Menges 1994). In light of these significant handicaps, college and university faculty are indeed confronted with a major task if they are to improve their teaching.

The goal of improving college teaching, though not necessarily novel (Cole 1978; Lee 1967), is certainly commendable. It is also related to some other significant issues in higher education, and perhaps foremost in the minds of educators is the consistent advancement of student learning. Learning is, after all, a primary goal of educational programs, and some have recently proposed that the focus of educational institutions should be shifted from teaching to learning (Barr and Tagg 1995; Cross 1996; O'Banion 1995–96). The challenge to improve student learning has been complicated, particularly in the past 20 years, as enrollments of college students have reflected more and more the diversity of our society. The influx of older students, displaced workers, minority students, females, commuter students—including those employed full-time—and other previously "nontraditional" student groups has placed unusual demands on institutions. In particular, these newer groups of students have emphasized the variability in student learning. Hence, a key to improving learning for all students is the recognition of the individuality of the learning process.

The public is also concerned about the extent of learning that is taking place in our institutions of higher education. Focusing on learning outcomes, the public demands institutional accountability, thus promoting a necessary emphasis on improving teaching. This development of excellence in teaching is particularly significant for the many faculty members who are inadequately prepared for their classroom responsibilities. A certain amount of professional pride accompanies the efforts of faculty, who are also concerned about student learning, as they strive to improve their performance. Unfortunately, efforts to improve teaching in higher education have often been resisted (Halpern 1994).

The Preparation of Faculty

The preparation of many college and university faculty for teaching has shortchanged them in at least four ways, as faculty have been deprived of the opportunity to understand how learning happens, to consider the use and value of feedback, to realize the importance of experimenting with teaching methods, and to review available resources for improving teaching and learning. Yet the inadequate preparation of faculty for the responsibilities of teaching is indicative of the typical lack of emphasis placed upon this faculty role in higher education (Schuster 1990, 1993). Characteristically, teaching has not been recognized as a necessary skill for college faculty (Halpern 1994; Menges 1994).

Graduate education for potential college and university faculty usually focuses on a concentration in the subject field and research applicable to this concentration. Generally speaking, few opportunities of any kind are offered to graduate students to provide them with pedagogical skills or techniques (Bass 1993; Boice 1992; Weimer 1990). In fact, the current emphasis in graduate study disparages any effort by potential college faculty to develop themselves as teachers (Eble 1983; Slevin 1993).

Thus, potential college faculty depend on the role models they encountered during their own instruction for the necessary exposure to instructional methodology (Lucas 1989). This dependence can lead to unfortunate methodological assumptions:

. . . that passive verbal transfer is an effective mode of instruction; that college students have long attention spans; that if teachers prepare well and keep talking nothing bad can happen; and that authority and truth reside in the figure behind the lectern (Eble 1988, p. 206).

Because the dominant method in their own experience was the lecture, college faculty have adopted this one method for the bulk of college teaching (Flood and Moll 1990). College faculty who believe that the lecture is still the most exciting and efficient method of teaching, however, may be surprised to discover just the opposite (Gardiner 1994; Halpern and Associates 1994). Moreover, with the increasing diversity of today's college students, their range of approaches to learning has similarly expanded. Yet faculty who have not had the opportunity to learn about the principles of teaching and learning may still contend that all students can learn the same ways they always have.

Based on their preparation, college and university faculty may believe that they can communicate the information in their subject fields because they have acquired extensive knowledge about the content. "A century ago the defining characteristic of pedagogical accomplishment was knowledge of content" (Shulman 1986, p. 7). Thus, college faculty were presumed capable of dispensing quantities of this content. While familiarity with the content is necessary, such knowledge is no longer adequate for teaching within a subject field (Svinicki 1990). As students have become more sophisticated and information continues to expand, teaching has become more than a process of dispensing a finite amount of information. The mere transmission of information is no longer sufficient for classroom instruction (Laws 1991). Even so, current practice continues to be dominated by presentational instructional practices that force students to remain passive learners (Wilson 1996).

Faculty have a responsibility to recognize the specific difficulties that students will have in understanding the content and then transform the content accordingly to enhance students' understanding (Shulman 1987). What is becoming increasingly clear is that educators need to reassess their purpose and function in the current information age (Hinchey 1995). In other words, whether or not teachers are willing to

Because the dominant method in their own experience was the lecture, college faculty have adopted this one method for the bulk of college teaching.

consider, adopt, and adapt various innovative instructional approaches, college teaching has already changed. Yet if teaching and learning are to improve in the college and university classroom, individual instructors must be willing to make the necessary changes (Svinicki 1990). Faculty likewise must be willing and eager learners themselves.

Efforts to Improve Teaching

The preparation of college faculty has not been ignored entirely. Some disciplines offer their graduate teaching assistants a course or seminar devoted to some of the principles of college teaching. In addition, both the Association of American Colleges and the American Association of Colleges and Universities have initiated projects that call attention to the need for better preparation of college teachers (Travis, Outlaw, and Reven 1996). Even before the efforts of these two organizations, a Doctor of Arts degree, whose expressed intent was to prepare graduate students for the requirements of college teaching, was developed and first offered at Carnegie-Mellon University. The Doctor of Arts, however, has not gained widespread acceptance and in fact has declined significantly in popularity since its inception (Glazer 1993).

A few institutions actually have increased the extent of teacher preparation programs for college faculty beyond the scope of the Doctor of Arts. Incorporating valuable instruction in learning theory and teaching methodology as well as practical internship experiences into existing master's and doctoral programs, over 20 colleges and universities nationwide offer graduate degrees in college teaching (Travis, Outlaw, and Reven 1996). Although all of these efforts are meeting a genuine need in preparing college faculty to teach, the clear majority of college instruction has not benefited from these programs.

Some well-meaning texts have been created to fill in the gaps left by graduate programs that do not include pedagogy (e.g., B. Davis 1993; Halpern and Associates 1994; McKeachie 1994; see Appendix A for a more complete reading list). And faculty members who are fortunate enough to have access to comprehensive faculty development programs could find yet another opportunity to supplement their preparation for teaching. A key element in many staff development programs has been an ongoing effort to collect and disseminate effective teaching strategies. Various projects and organizations, including the Professional and Organizational Development Network in Higher Education, the National Institute for Staff and Organizational Development, the National Center on Postsecondary Teaching, Learning, and Assessment, and the National Center for Research to Improve Postsecondary Teaching and Learning, also have demonstrated their commitment to such an effort.

Among the numerous strategies created to assist in the improvement of teaching, some have been developed on a sound research base to apply across the disciplines of college teaching. Hence, these strategies have reached a degree of sophistication sufficient to differentiate them as teaching improvement "models." This distinction suggests that each model has a thorough foundation in the rich literature on teaching and learning and has been tested in an actual teaching environment. Moreover, teaching improvement models are not merely classroom methods, such as lecture or simulation, but have been designed to augment the use of various teaching strategies and methods. The collective purpose of such models essentially has been to foster improvement in the quality of college teaching.

Although each model may be singularly different and attract a specific clientele among faculty and administrators, the tendency to group these models for discussion and selection, much like a menu, is rare. Through the activities of various faculty development programs and organizations, some information about these models might have been collected, but the typical faculty development effort often tends to be an endorsement of only one or two of the applicable models. Generally selected to be presented to instructors through faculty development workshops, this limited array of teaching improvement models might not be sufficient to offer faculty members what they need. Many faculty members simply may not have sufficient time to attend such workshops merely to sample the models presented so they can select one for their personal use. A more comprehensive and concise compilation of teaching improvement models is lacking. Hence, faculty need such a "menu" to facilitate their consideration, adoption, and adaptation of the model or models they perceive as most useful in meeting their own circumstances.

Models for Improving College Teaching

This report presents a collection of selected models to provide college and university faculty with a range of different approaches to improve instructional practice. While not all-inclusive, this assortment of models offers an initial resource for faculty interested in improving their teaching and their students' learning. The collection includes a total of 16 models, each one briefly described with accompanying critical reviews, where available, from the literature. Each model has been selected for its utility to individual faculty members, its complete, specific structure, and the accessible reference literature (providing faculty the opportunity to pursue additional information for a particular model).

Essentially, these models are suggested to fill a gap in the preparation of college faculty and to offer specific procedures or ideas that can be implemented easily without formalized training. The entire collection is categorized according to the ultimate purpose of the respective models. In addition to the selected models described in each category, related techniques, which are lacking in specific definition or not appreciably developed in the literature, are briefly discussed.

The six categories of models are arranged to facilitate faculty members' use of this collection. Based on a presumption that most faculty would prefer to review and consider models that are relatively easy and quick in application, the collection begins with a category of models designed for self-examination of the teaching process. The following category of models provides for sharing with colleagues. The sharing process continues and expands to include institutions and organizations across the country in the third category. While sharing is also part of the fourth category, the model focuses on the learning of teaching skills and requires specific resources, especially trained facilitators. Beginning with the fifth category, the models provide a theoretical basis for the teaching and learning process, concluding with theories of instructional design. For newer faculty especially, one or more of the last three categories may be particularly useful for filling in the gaps left by inadequate preparation. Veteran faculty, on the other hand, may prefer to try the more self-directed approaches of the first three categories.

Unless faculty routinely videotape their classes, obtaining feedback to assess one's teaching may not be easy. Classroom observation by a peer or administrator is often only an occasional opportunity that also can be threatening. Because all faculty who seek to improve their teaching require ample feedback on classroom activities, the first category includes models designed to assist the faculty member in collecting feedback for assessing instruction. Hence, the first group of models is referred to as *assessment/feedback models*. The Classroom Assessment model, created by Angelo and Cross and already widely used among community college faculty, is an example of a procedure to elicit feedback for the purpose of assessing teaching and learning. Although faculty development can almost always benefit from sanction or support from the organization, each model in this category is also suited to individual and independent application by faculty members, without the specific requirement of institutional support.

The next category, *discussion/sharing models,* includes endeavors that provide faculty with an event and an environment especially conducive to sharing ideas among fellow faculty members. The benefits of collaboration, whether fostered through formal programs like the Great Teachers Seminar or Academic Alliances or through more informal means, are considered some of the most influential aspects of faculty development. Unlike assessment/feedback models, these models naturally require the participation of others, although informal collaboration still does not depend on institutional support.

In addition to faculty members' sharing their ideas with one another directly or individually, some models have been developed for sharing or disseminating these ideas to a wide audience of faculty. Hence, the Center for Improving Teaching and three different publications are grouped together as *dissemination models*. Relying more heavily on institutional support, these models, like this report, are intended to dispense an extensive assortment of ideas to the largest possible audience.

Because many faculty members have not had the benefit of developing teaching skills before beginning a teaching career, the section on *clinical development models* describes an in-service opportunity to experiment without negative consequences. The Instructional Skills Workshop uses a laboratory setting common to teacher preparation programs but depends on institutional support for implementation.

This report presents a collection of selected models to provide college and university faculty with a range of different approaches to improve instructional practice.

With this model, faculty actually have the opportunity to practice short lessons using previously untried methods.

In addition to methodological preparation, teacher preparation programs also focus on learning theory. With the advent of the concepts of learning styles and multiple intelligences, the theoretical basis for understanding the process of learning has become even more important for the practicing educator. Unlike the typical educational psychology class, however, *teaching/learning models* do not dwell on the theories themselves but instead offer theoretical bases for understanding how to improve practice. For example, Anderson's Adaptive Control of Thinking not only describes the learning process, but also presents specific procedures to facilitate specific types of learning. For professors lost without the lecture, DuBois's Learning Strategy Training can help lecturers design better-organized presentations as well as teach students how to organize their note taking. The extensive research on varying learning styles and intelligences is represented in Lazear's model for applying multiple intelligences to teaching, Kolb's Dimensions of Learning, the 4MAT training program, and Grasha's integration of teaching and learning styles.

For the new faculty member, instructional planning is often an abbreviated exercise between unpacking in a new residence and walking into class on the first day. Without the experience of developing trial plans in a teacher preparation program, faculty members can find themselves following a trial-and-error process that may last for several semesters. Both Gagné's Instructional Event Design and Diamond's Educational Program Development, represented among *instructional planning models,* can help the faculty member pace through the necessary process of course and lesson planning.

This collection is, understandably, relatively limited. The models appended to five of the categories are evidence of additional techniques, many of which may lack the specificity or the research base that has been incorporated in the identification of the 16 models described in this volume. And similar models are undoubtedly in the process of development. Yet this collection should provide faculty members eager to improve their college teaching with a place to start.

Still, these models are not a silver bullet designed to solve all the problems inherent in college teaching. As with any initiative to improve something, the efforts should continue incrementally. Clearly, not every model will prove successful for every faculty member. Faculty should begin by reflecting on their own knowledge of teaching and learning, then select the category and model that seem to meet a perceived need. Improvement necessitates a certain amount of experimentation as well, so some models might have to be tried and discarded later. Finally, efforts to improve college teaching should proceed without an expectation of perfection— only with a commitment simply to improve college teaching and learning continuously.

Faculty who teach in addition to their myriad other responsibilities and are serious about instructional development usually are careful about how they expend their valuable available time. Hence, to assist faculty in reviewing and selecting these models, the illustration of each model is brief and to the point. The reader should therefore not expect to find a complex theoretical discourse or an in-depth, analytical treatise demonstrating the relationship among the models being described. But this resource should simplify the process of improving one's teaching for the already busy faculty member.

In essence, this monograph is targeted directly to faculty to assist them in making individual choices for developing their own instruction. Faculty are encouraged to consider all of the available models for improving teaching in light of their own objectives. Although helpful advice from peers and others may facilitate decision making, faculty must be allowed to maintain ownership of their application of these and other instructional interventions.

ASSESSMENT/FEEDBACK MODELS

The use of assessment to improve instruction has been attempted at all levels of schooling and with a wide range of techniques, both formative and summative. Instructional assessment conducted by the faculty member to provide specific feedback that the instructor can retain can be particularly useful to college and university faculty. This feedback "is most effective if it is not made public and if it emphasizes competencies instead of comparisons" (Cross 1990, p. 124). Such assessment can target specific instructional criteria or particular problems perceived by the instructor.

Every good teacher conducts some continuous form of self-assessment of instruction. Perhaps the most significant contribution of faculty-conducted assessment is the establishment of a process to improve teaching and learning, an advantage that traditional evaluation procedures propose to offer but rarely do. The models presented in this section provide four approaches to eliciting feedback that will inform instructional decision making. The first two models offer assessment procedures that focus on the teaching process as a whole. Also addressing the entire process, the third model includes defined components for making changes to improve teaching. Finally, the section describes an assessment model designed for taking action, which has more specific applications.

Faculty Inventory of Good Practice

Faculty self-assessment can be an effective source of feedback for the faculty member seeking to improve practice. Chickering and Gamson (1987) provided the substance for such a process of generating feedback with research that generated the development of an assessment model for faculty. The model's development began with a Wingspread Conference, sponsored by the Johnson Foundation, in 1986. At the conference, Chickering and Gamson organized a task force that included Alexander W. Astin, Howard Bowen, William Boyd, Carol M. Boyer, K. Patricia Cross, Kenneth Eble, Russell Edgerton, Jerry Gaff, Henry Halsted, Joseph Katz, C. Robert Pace, Marvin W. Peterson, and Richard C. Richardson, Jr. As a result of the work of this task force at the conference and during the months that followed, Chickering and Gamson presented Seven Principles for Good Practice in Undergraduate Education (1987).

Seven Principles for Good Practice
In Undergraduate Education

The Seven Principles provide a basic, general description of the optimum classroom behaviors for effective learning. Grounded on research conducted by the task force on successful teaching and learning behaviors in higher education, the list of principles included common sense themes, not couched in educational jargon:

> *Good practice in undergraduate education: (1) encourages contacts between students and faculty, (2) develops reciprocity and cooperation among students, (3) uses active learning techniques, (4) gives prompt feedback, (5) emphasizes time on task, (6) communicates high expectations, (7) respects diverse talents and ways of learning* (Chickering and Gamson 1987, p. 3).

While this list may appear somewhat simplistic, almost suggesting a set of laws for education, the authors insist that no such implication was intended, asserting that the principles simply should assist the process of improving teaching and learning by providing guidance to educators, students, and governing officials (Chickering and Gamson 1987). Essentially, this purpose—to develop college instruction—and the inherent simplicity of the list are primary reasons for their inclusion in this collection of teaching improvement models.

The principles are based on "50 years of research on the way teachers teach and students learn" (Chickering and Gamson 1987, p. 4). Student and faculty interaction understandably should affect the learning process, whether in the classroom or not, particularly because of its strong impact on students' motivation. Collaborative learning efforts among students are similarly influential and much more successful than a consistent dependence on competition in the classroom. Learning is also enhanced if students are given the opportunity to actively participate in the process, which is one of the most frequent criticisms of the passive lecture technique.

Maintaining students' motivation depends on feedback that informs students of their progress in learning. Using tests to analyze students' errors, while not stressed in our educational system, is one approach to feedback that can foster effective learning. "Time on task" refers to focusing students' attention on a particular subject or learning activity; few people would argue that attentiveness to learning tasks will yield increased learning. Expectations of students' achievement can produce a variety of responses from students based on the variations of their personalities and learning styles, yet students generally respond favorably to educators who have confidence in their capability to succeed. The inherent diversity of students and their approaches to learning therefore demand attentiveness from faculty.

Each principle can be used individually, yet they tend to be synergistic, providing results that are much greater when applied collectively (Chickering and Gamson 1987). Thus, the Seven Principles suggest a recurring theme for teaching improvement models: While individual techniques and procedures may be effective, the combined efforts of a unified system or model can be much more powerful. The Seven Principles "employ six powerful forces in education: activity, cooperation, diversity, expectations, interaction, responsibility" (Chickering and Gamson 1987, p. 4). Each force, like the Seven Principles that involve them, demonstrates a strength in the teaching and learning process. Hence, learning can be enhanced with active techniques, cooperative student efforts, individual differences, students' anticipated success, sharing between students and faculty, and an acceptance of expected behavior.

The faculty inventory

After completing their work on the original list of principles, Chickering and Gamson responded to continued interest in the Seven Principles by developing two inventories, one for individual faculty and the other for institutions, to measure compliance with the principles. The two inventories were published by the Johnson Foundation in 1989, and the entire initial printing of 40,000 copies was distributed in a week (Chickering and Gamson 1991). Total distribution of the inventories exceeded 500,000 copies by 1991. The faculty inventory is designed for the personal use of instructors who wish to improve their teaching. Although such an instrument can easily be misused for summative evaluation, results from such abuse of the inventories would not be valid (Chickering and Gamson 1991).

The faculty inventory is divided into seven segments, directly applicable to the Seven Principles. Each segment includes 10 statements relating to faculty behaviors that require responses using a five-point scale: very often, often, occasionally, rarely, and never. For example, one of the statements in segment 6 is "I make clear my expectations orally and in writing at the beginning of each course" (Chickering, Gamson, and Barsi 1989, p. 9). Considering this statement, a faculty member might indicate that the behavior is demonstrated occasionally.

Upon completing each segment, as well as the entire inventory, faculty have the opportunity to reflect on specific areas for improvement. In fact, the entire inventory is a tool for faculty reflection on practice. Using the example cited above, the faculty member who indicates occasional demonstration of the behavior for this one statement would be expected to reflect on the desirability of increasing this behavior. If other items in the same category are also practiced infrequently, the faculty member is expected to react with concern and make a concerted effort to increase the frequency of the desirable activities. This type of review of the entire inventory should offer faculty members significant insight into personal instructional practice.

Because the faculty inventory is designed to be self-administered, faculty have the opportunity to select specific issues indicated by the instrument for attention and/or intervention. Faculty should be cautioned, however, to avoid the temptation to attempt action on multiple concerns after completing the inventory. Efforts to improve one's teaching should be initiated gradually to ensure greater success. Such a cautious approach to implementing the Seven Principles should provide faculty with a sustained agenda for improving teaching and learning.

Inventories as contributors to good practice

The initial publication of the Seven Principles created so much interest that *Wingspread Journal* republished them three months later, and the Johnson Foundation provided over 150,000 copies of the article at no charge during the following 18 months (Chickering and Gamson 1991). Reprints were also published in a number of other publications, including *University Affairs* (Canada) and the newsletters of the American Association of State Colleges and Universities and various teaching improvement centers at higher education institutions.

References in the literature to the Seven Principles and the inventories likewise illustrate the impact of Chickering and Gamson's work. "The most widely known and applied" variables influencing college learning "are the Seven Principles for Good Practice in Undergraduate Education" (Angelo 1996, p. 60). The inventories have been the catalyst for numerous faculty discussions (Centra 1993). The National Center for Education Statistics (1994) included the Seven Principles in its discussion of potential "good practice" indicators. Another recent publication, *The Seven Principles in Action* (Hatfield 1995), highlights case studies of the principles in use at over 75 colleges and universities across the nation. An earlier study (Poulsen 1991) of the use of the Seven Principles among private colleges, public universities, and community colleges yielded generally positive responses.

The Seven Principles have been cited as a basic approach to the knowledge of pedagogy faculty need (Dinham 1996). Yet another endorsement of the Seven Principles emphasizes the correlation between the principles and program improvement (Krueger 1993). "Regardless of the assessment tools utilized, linking the program to Chickering and Gamson's seven principles and constantly asking the question 'How can we improve?' provide the kind of focus needed to effect genuine improvement" (p. 273). Some say "no better list of fundamental principles" can be found (Frederick 1989, p. 32).

Moreover, based on the number of inventories distributed by the Johnson Foundation, the faculty inventory has been recognized as a helpful diagnostic tool. A wide range of possible uses of the instrument also demonstrates its flexibility and utility (Barsi 1991). Clearly, the faculty inventory is an important faculty development tool that can be implemented easily and quickly. Both the inventory and the Seven Principles are still available from the Seven Principles Resource Center at Winona State University in Minnesota (see Appendix B for the address).

The initial publication of the Seven Principles created so much interest that Wingspread Journal republished them three months later, and the Johnson Foundation provided over 150,000 copies of the article at no charge during the following 18 months.

Two-Dimensional Model of Effective College Teaching

Assessment in the context of effectiveness indicators can clearly enable faculty to begin improving their teaching. A measurement of two specific skills in college teaching can help a faculty member discover the essence of effective teaching (Lowman 1984): the faculty member's ability to develop intellectual excitement and the ability to generate interpersonal rapport among students (see also Lowman 1995 for a defining set of characteristic adjectives that help to describe the instructor who elicits intellectual excitement or interpersonal rapport). While both skills should enhance teaching no matter what the situation or students, faculty who are able to master even one of the skills will have some impact in particular situations.

Intellectual excitement

Students' involvement in the learning process depends upon their attitudinal commitment to the endeavor. Students can develop intellectual excitement if a faculty member is a master of both the subject matter and the various methods available for teaching and learning. To evoke intellectual excitement, an instructor needs to clearly communicate the content in a manner that will engender positive student reactions (Lowman 1984). Simply knowing and sharing information does not enhance learning. The information must be delivered in a format that students can sufficiently understand and interpret. Thus, the instructor also should be cognizant of the aspects of the content that may interfere with students' comprehension.

Further, teaching and learning, like any acts of communication, can be hampered by interference, both within the individual student and in the surrounding environment. To block out such interfering distractions, instructors need to use communication strategies that will keep their listeners focused and maintain their attention on the content even after the class is over—although the efforts to maintain students' involvement must not be reduced to performing for entertainment.

Levels of intellectual excitement can be high, moderate, and low (Lowman 1984). An instructor who elicits a low level of intellectual excitement may be obscure or uninteresting. The moderate level suggests a minimal degree of intelligibility and excitement, while the high level naturally indicates a command of both qualities. The faculty member who creates a high level of intellectual excitement might be described as enthusiastic, knowledgeable, and/or inspiring. An instructor's mastery of intellectual excitement is especially critical, as the focus is on the content and methods for its delivery.

Interpersonal rapport

Although the learning process may be considered chiefly cognitive in nature, the affective domain is also an integral part of the operation. Student learning can be adversely affected by unjust practices, authoritarian attitudes, or negative feedback from the instructor. Similarly, faculty can be intimidated by students' expectations and the outcomes of evaluations that depend on students' test scores. Awareness of these drawbacks and the necessary abilities to overcome their influence are the domain of interpersonal rapport. Faculty can excel in this dimension by inhibiting nonproductive attitudes and reinforcing constructive ones.

Like intellectual excitement, the dimension of interpersonal rapport is characterized by high, moderate, and low levels. Students might regard the faculty member who maintains a low level of interpersonal rapport as erratic, domineering, or insensitive. At the moderate level, instructors tend to suggest a more open and friendly attitude. Highly sensitive, orderly, and tolerant faculty would therefore be considered to also exhibit a high level of interpersonal rapport. While the dimension of intellectual excitement is especially critical to the learning process, interpersonal rapport might not be considered equally important. College faculty will probably not uniformly agree that a more humanistic instructor is consequently more effective. Students, on the other hand, have indicated their preference for instructors who succeed with interpersonal rapport (Lowman 1984).

Lowman's revised text (1995) provides additional detail for the interpersonal dimension. Recognizing some differences within this dimension, Lowman split it into the more specific areas of interpersonal concern and effective motivation, concluding that faculty who demonstrate concern for students might not necessarily exhibit motivating behaviors and vice versa. Lowman added this distinction only in the second dimension, however, to provide a more thorough understanding of interpersonal rapport; he did not maintain this differentiation in the unified model described in the following paragraphs.

Intersecting dimensions

The complete model, with the three levels of each dimension, was further incorporated into a nine-cell grid that provides a full graphic picture of the concept (see figure 1). As each level of a dimension intersects with another on the grid, a different result is indicated for the faculty member. Hence, instruction that is low in both intellectual excitement and interpersonal rapport would be considered insufficient, because the instructor can neither present the material nor motivate the students sufficiently. Such an instructor would be considered least effective (Lowman 1984). In contrast, instruction registering high in both intellectual excitement and interpersonal rapport would be considered exceptional. Faculty at this combination of levels are regarded most effective (Lowman 1984).

FIGURE 1

GRID OF EFFECTIVE INSTRUCTION

	HIGH	Content-Centered	Traditional	Exceptional
Intellectual Excitement	**MODERATE**	Sufficient	Ample	Pragmatic
	LOW	Deficient	Mediocre	Student-Centered
	LOW		**MODERATE**	**HIGH**

Interpersonal Rapport

Source: Suggested by Lowman's (1984) Two-Dimensional Model.

In a sense, Lowman's model is similar to much of the research on learning styles that offers relative categories that attempt to describe most of the learning tendencies of most students. Likewise, the nine generalized categories in Lowman's Two-Dimensional Model do not necessarily describe every faculty member (Lowman 1995). Instructors can be described by characteristics of more than one category. And students can still learn, even if faculty tend to be "deficient."

Defining the dimensions
The Two-Dimensional Model demonstrates with this grid its similarity to two theories of management or leadership: the Managerial Grid (Blake and Mouton 1985), which depicts management behavior according to concern for people and concern for production, ranging from low to high on each axis of the grid; and two types of leadership style that depict both relationship and task behaviors along two dimensions ranging from low to high (Hersey and Blanchard 1982). Thus, the foundation of Lowman's work can be further substantiated in theoretical administrative research.

Lowman's model has been cited as a way to determine and develop effective teaching (Lucas 1994). Others have found it "appealing and very persuasive" (Fink 1989, p. 27).

The organization of the information in the model is clear and provides an effective schema for a self-evaluation of one's own efforts to attain a successful blend of intellectual impact and emotional support for the complex kinds of mastery that dominate the college classroom. . . . Intellectual excitement and interpersonal rapport become the constructs that fuel our existence as academicians. Lowman has given us a useful and excellent guide for the journey we must take to fulfill our obligations to the students we teach (Mathis 1984, pp. 51–52).

The combination of practical advice and theoretical support was noted as a highlight in Lowman's efforts (McCaslin 1985), which persuade the instructor to think and respond (McNinch 1985).

Some, however, have been more critical of the model, citing limitations in the model's reliance on teaching methods like the lecture and on a set of specific descriptors of effective faculty (Centra 1993). "Good teaching is more complicated than any list of qualities or characteristics can suggest" (p. 41). Another possible weakness of Lowman's model is that it does not include an inventory to help faculty conduct a self-assessment like Chickering and Gamson's faculty inventory, and determining the degrees of excitement and rapport exhibited by an instructor could therefore be a difficult task. Yet Lowman (1984) suggested by his own determinations that subjective judgments can be made about one's particular placement on the two-dimensional grid. And Lowman's list of descriptive adjectives (1995) should also help faculty in making more informed decisions.

The Five-Step Process for Improving Teaching

Yet another technique for self-assessment combines assessment with action steps to yield a systematic approach to assess instruction and implement change as an instructional improvement process (Weimer 1990). Not unlike a common decision-making action cycle, Weimer's model incorporates five stages: awareness, information retrieval, selection of alternatives, implementation of plan, and evaluation. The cyclical nature of this model reflects Weimer's assertion that teaching cannot be improved overall with a singular effort or with individual tips or ideas: A more systematic approach to developing instruction is necessary (Weimer 1990).

Like all the models described in this section, the Five-Step Process is designed for the exclusive use of the individual faculty member. Although colleagues and teaching specialists may be consulted as resources, the evaluative data and resulting actions remain the sole province of the instructor. Weimer's model is also presented in a format that offers additional suggestions for dealing with specific aspects of instructional development (1990). Each stage of the model focuses on a specific purpose and incorporates distinctive procedures to consider for accomplishing that purpose. Some faculty members may discover other strategies in addition to those Weimer recommends for accomplishing each goal.

Awareness

Understandably, faculty need to begin with an understanding of their own approach to teaching. In this initial stage of the process, therefore, the faculty member conducts an instructional self-evaluation. Among the possible means for personally examining one's teaching behaviors is the use of videotaped examples of actual teaching. A relatively common technique that has been studied extensively, videotaping one's teaching can provide substantial feedback (Davis 1993; Krupnick 1987; Lowman 1995). Reflecting about the teaching process is also helpful and is an essential skill that effective instructors typically develop.

Weimer suggests using one or more checklists as well as additional background reading to assist faculty in reflection. Some relatively simple questionnaires and checklists (Weimer 1987, 1990; Weimer, Parrett, and Kerns 1988), somewhat similar to the faculty inventory in Chickering and Gamson's model, help the faculty member to focus on specific behaviors in the classroom. One of Weimer's checklists (1990) inquires about the instructor's hand and body movements, posture, rate and volume of speech, and facial expressions. Finally, using a technique common to evaluation, faculty can examine their syllabi and other teaching materials, whether or not in portfolio format.

Information retrieval

Self-evaluation may provide a somewhat one-sided perspective of teaching, and additional information is therefore needed from others who might present differing viewpoints. Feedback from students can be extremely illuminating (Angelo and Cross 1993), and both current and former students should be asked to provide useful feedback (Weimer 1990). A wide range of techniques and forms designed to elicit this necessary feedback is available (Angelo and Cross 1993; Murray 1987; Weimer, Parrett, and Kerns 1988). Colleagues could also be a source of information. Through discussions, sharing of teaching materials, and classroom observation, faculty can gain additional insight from other instructors and academic leaders. Workshops, classes, and supplementary reading can, in addition, augment the information already acquired.

Selection of alternatives

Once sufficient information has been gathered, the faculty member needs to determine what can and should be changed in the instructional process. These changes are based on the information obtained as well as existing objectives. Instructors also need to decide how to make these changes. Gradual, step-by-step changes may be preferred. The available options for changing instruction are usually numerous (Weimer 1990).

Implementation of plan

After selecting the desired changes, the faculty member puts the plan into action. The success of the plan depends on an organized and enthusiastic effort by the faculty member (Weimer 1990). Faculty need to maintain control of the process, so a moderate approach may be necessary to avoid undue stress. The desired results should not be rushed.

Evaluation

A necessary step in any implementation of change is an evaluation of the results. This stage might include additional gathering of information, both personally and from others, as in the first two stages of the model. This information is needed to determine whether the desired results have been achieved. If the chosen plan is not sufficiently successful, additional changes may need to be considered, selected, and attempted, thus continuing the entire cycle once again. Completing the cycle with an evaluation of any further changes is always recommended.

The five steps' influence on improvement

The flexibility of this model, as a result of its basic simplicity, is a major advantage. Weimer (1990) has supported the Five-Step Process with an extensive research base, incorporating some important concerns to complement the model. For example, certain elements are key in the improvement of teaching, such as continuous efforts to gather feedback and assess progress, consideration of several improvement strategies, faculty collaboration, and, of course, administrative support. In addition, some institutional alternatives should be available to support the improvement process, including an administrator designated to serve as a faculty consultant, a faculty development committee, and a program for faculty development that includes an office, a resource center, and/or a director.

But while improvement is possible, the process may not necessarily be simple (Weimer 1990). If the process begins with an identification of inadequate faculty who need to improve, the potential for success will be diminished. Some inaccurate faculty suppositions can also be obstacles to improvement. Such ideas as "a knowledge of content is the only necessity for teaching," "good teaching is an inherited skill," and "subject matter is more important than the student" are common misconceptions. The profession's lack of commitment to adequate instructional preparation and faculty opposition to efforts at improvement are two of the most serious obstacles (Weimer 1990).

References to Weimer's model clearly indicate a recognition of her work. Her efforts have been called "excellent directives for improving teaching" (Boice 1992, p. 9) and "a good example of accumulated progress in [instructional development]" (p. 133). Her plan for gathering feedback is "exemplary" (p. 150).

Consider two examples of her clear thinking and expertise, typical of [instructional development] writing. One is the concept of instructional awareness; most faculty benefit from beginning with overdue reflections on how they teach as an initial step in becoming better teachers. Another is a stepwise plan for improving teaching. It begins with instructional awareness and includes informal feedback and setting goals for change (Boice 1992, p. 133).

Weimer helped to establish "that most faculty can benefit from reflection on how they teach as a beginning step in becoming better teachers," underlining the importance of instructional awareness in improving teaching (Lucas 1994, p. 102). Weimer's checklist (included in an appendix) is a helpful approach in developing this awareness. It is an exercise that "allows faculty to detach themselves from their teaching to look at their own behaviors" (p. 132). Weimer's model is useful to follow in collecting data to improve teaching (Lewis 1991).

Weimer has been called "the best-known and most articulate source of information on instructional development in this country" (Chism 1991, p. 237), emphasizing the importance of her model as a contribution to the literature on improving teaching (see also Humphreys 1990; Kingston 1991; Puyear 1990). Implementing Weimer's model is certainly worth the effort (Moore 1990).

Classroom Assessment

Based on the assumption that information from students relating to their learning progress can help faculty adapt their instruction to meet students' needs, Angelo and Cross (1993) developed a multifaceted approach for gathering feedback from students. With techniques like minute papers, student goal ranking, and focused listing, Classroom Assessment is possibly the most flexible and readily usable of the models presented in this report. In fact, the use of any one of Cross and Angelo's techniques does not require formal training, funding, or even considerable time.

The return on such a limited investment, however, can be surprising. Faculty and students both can find an increased sense of empowerment with this new access to information and opportunity to be heard. Even the timid student who is disinclined to speak up in class can have a voice with this method. While establishing these vitally important communication links between faculty and students, Classroom Assessment begins a process to improve teaching and learning.

Weimer helped to establish "that most faculty can benefit from reflection on how they teach as a beginning step in becoming better teachers," underlining the importance of instructional awareness in improving teaching.

Further, the use of Classroom Assessment permits this improvement during the instructional process so that students can receive immediate attention to their learning difficulties.

The classroom research project

Angelo and Cross began the classroom research project in 1988 with grants from the Ford Foundation and Pew Charitable Trusts (Angelo 1990). Their initial work for the project, however, was the development of their Teaching Goals Inventory (TGI) in 1986 (Angelo and Cross 1993). They designed the TGI to help faculty members focus on their instructional goals through self-assessment. Considered the initial step for faculty who wish to begin classroom assessment, the TGI is intended to help each faculty member individualize the perceived goals for each course, determine assessment techniques to measure how instruction is meeting these goals, and initiate a process of sharing these goal perceptions with other faculty (Angelo and Cross 1993).

The revised TGI includes 52 items, listed as goals for students, such as "develop ability to concentrate" and "develop a lifelong love of learning" (Angelo and Cross 1993, pp. 394–95). Faculty indicate their perception of each goal's importance on a five-point scale ranging from essential (5) to not applicable (1). An additional item on the inventory requests an identification of the instructor's chief teaching role, such as "teaching subject matter" or "serving as a role model." A scoring device accompanying the revised TGI provides faculty with the opportunity to personally tally responses in six categories—thinking skills, academic skills, subject knowledge, general education, vocational training, and personal improvement (Angelo and Cross 1993).

The classroom research project incorporated research dealing with educational objectives and formative evaluation (Bloom 1956; Bloom, Hastings, and Madaus 1971). Formative evaluation, as distinct from summative evaluation, is designed primarily to provide indicators for improvement rather than some type of summary judgment. Angelo and Cross also used numerous syntheses of research on higher education's impact on students, such as Astin (1977), Feldman and Newcomb (1969), and Pace (1979). Essentially, the project focused on three major initiatives: refining the TGI, fostering teacher-directed assessment through the development of classroom assessment techniques, and encouraging the expansion of classroom assessment into instructional research to heighten understanding and to improve the process of teaching and learning (Angelo 1990; Angelo and Cross 1989, 1993). The concept of classroom research involves the commitment of an entire institution to continuous data gathering on classroom practice and experience to inform both faculty and administrators in their efforts to improve teaching and learning. (Because classroom research is an institutional program, it is not detailed in this report.)

The issue of classroom research was an overarching theme of the project that sought to identify faculty as researchers of the instructional process. Classroom research, as distinct from traditional research conducted by university professors, is concerned more with a search for understanding about successful classroom practices than with generalizable predictor schemes (Cross 1990). Thus, the practicality of the project is its major feature.

Classroom assessment techniques
Angelo and Cross developed the basis for the Classroom Assessment model, 30 relatively simple classroom assessment techniques (CATs), during the early stages of the classroom research project. Expanded and redesigned into an even simpler and more accessible format, the 1993 edition of the CATs offers techniques for assessing students' skills and knowledge; attitudes, values, and self-awareness; and reactions to instruction. Angelo and Cross actually ranked each CAT according to the perceived difficulty and time commitment required.

Based on the principles of formative assessment, the CATs afford faculty members the opportunity to focus on interventions to assist students in the learning process (Angelo and Cross 1993). The techniques are designed primarily to provide faculty and students with valuable feedback and the extended opportunity for dialogue. Aside from summative assessments, such as traditional testing, faculty rarely have the opportunity to elicit needed feedback from their students. Further, much feedback from tests tends to be too little and too late. Faculty need input from students during the process of instruction to discover the problems students might be having with learning while the difficulties can still be corrected.

In addition to its formative nature, Classroom Assessment focuses on the learner and is managed by the individual faculty member (Angelo and Cross 1993). The development of learning skills among students, rather than the renewal of teaching, is the aim of the model. Moreover, faculty members are best suited for collecting formative data and acting on the results. "The teacher is not obliged to share the results of Classroom Assessment with anyone outside the classroom" (p. 4). Although their use is specific to each classroom and situation, the techniques can be adapted for application in any discipline.

Angelo and Cross (1993) identified some fundamental assumptions for their Classroom Assessment model, based on their extensive research during the course of the project, that link the model with improved teaching and learning. These assumptions take into consideration that both faculty and students need feedback. Using the techniques can also aid professional development. Perhaps most important, however, "Classroom Assessment does not require specialized training; it can be carried out by dedicated teachers from all disciplines" (p. 10).

While the TGI can help a faculty member focus on generalized instructional goals, teachers may need to relate specific goals to specific lessons or classes and to focus on further information that is needed. Thus, they can achieve a more immediate link to the CATs. To serve as an additional instrument for this purpose, figure 2 is a simplified questionnaire that offers faculty yet another ready mode of access to the CATs. An alternative to beginning an assessment project with teaching goals is to begin with questions (Angelo and Cross 1993).

FIGURE 2

QUESTIONNAIRE FOR PLANNING CLASSROOM ASSESSMENT: DISCOVERING GOALS

1. What class (or lesson) do you teach (or have taught) that you believe can be improved?
2. What are three specific strengths of the class (or lesson)?
3. What is at least one weakness?
4. Describe the way your students learn.
5. What additional information from students do you need to help them learn?

A sample of four CATs is briefly described to give readers an idea of the nature and purpose of the entire collection of techniques. They were selected because of their relative simplicity for implementation. Understandably, faculty new to the model will have greater initial success with some of the less complex CATs, such as the following techniques.

One of the CATs that seems to have achieved the widest use, perhaps because of its extreme simplicity and obvious utility, is the "minute paper." Presumably the creation of a physics professor at the University of California–Berkeley (Wilson 1986), the minute paper has become a familiar technique (Davis 1993). It is also a good example of the common nature of many of the assessment techniques, which "probably have been invented and reinvented time and again by instructors in various colleges at different times" (Angelo and Cross 1993, p. 153).

The minute paper simply involves two questions developed by the instructor that will cause students to reflect on specific aspects of a day's lesson. The questions usually focus on a student's impression of the most significant aspect of the lesson and a question that remains in the student's mind at the end of the lesson (Angelo and Cross 1993). Thus, the minute paper provides the instructor with two very valuable insights into the immediate learning process: comprehension of the content as well as lingering difficulties with it. This kind of information in advance of any testing can clearly benefit both student and teacher.

Another technique is "goal ranking and matching." A procedure usually reserved for the initial meetings of a class, goal ranking is intended to compare students' goals for the class and the potential for their achievement with those of the instructor (Angelo and Cross 1993). Faculty members' success with this technique depends on their flexibility, as students' goals may not always match those of the instructor. Additionally, students' goals may not be readily applicable to the cognitive aspects of the class. Often, students admit that their primary goal is to pass the class, as opposed to a specific learning goal. Consequently, faculty using this technique should caution students to focus on actual learning objectives.

Similar to the minute paper in focusing on students' specific conceptualizations is a technique called "focused listing." By asking students to list a group of key concepts related to a specific topic, the instructor can draw students' attention to a major course topic while discovering the level of conceptual understanding among the students in class (Angelo and Cross 1993). The list can be prepared to check students' reading or listening or to precede a lesson simply to draw students' attention to the subject matter. A variation of this technique can be used as a pretest or post-test to note students' preparation for the course as well as to measure overall achievement.

While focused listing can be used to quickly check students' understanding of reading assignments, the "reading rating" technique provides the instructor with additional helpful information about the text itself. Selecting good textbooks that are directly applicable to college courses is often frustrating, and although some technologists suggest that textbooks may one day become obsolete, the task of text selection remains for now. The fact that many students may not understand some printed texts as well as instructors do should not come as a complete shock to most faculty members. Even the circumstance that some students do not read at all, while disappointing, is not unusual. The reading rating is designed to provide faculty with information on their students' reading as well as their understanding and satisfaction with a specific reading assignment (Angelo and Cross 1993). Thus, a faculty member can supplement gaps in understanding for the current class and make a more informed selection of readings or text the next time the class is offered.

A few cautionary suggestions may be necessary for those who are ready to try some of these techniques for the first time. The amount of information resulting from using just one technique in one class two or three times in a semester may be significant. Hence, faculty are advised to begin classroom assessment slowly and with relatively simple techniques (Angelo and Cross 1993) so they are assured of manageable amounts of useful information. Faculty should also allow more time than anticipated when first attempting classroom assessment (Angelo and Cross 1993).

Second, this process of gathering anonymous feedback from students may be new to them, and instructors should therefore make allowances to ensure their successful participation in classroom assessment. Students may need specific instructions to complete a given technique as well as an introduction to the model itself. To ensure students' honesty and seriousness, the desired approach, faculty should insist on anonymity, even through the use of index cards for replies. And faculty need to respond promptly to the feedback, with an indication of potential solutions to learning problems (Angelo and Cross 1993). Students will believe that their input is being taken seriously only if the dialogue is a two-way street and appropriate action follows.

Perhaps the most unusual feature of Classroom Assessment, when compared to many "teacherproof" techniques that have been developed, is its adaptability. Techniques are offered as suggestions rather than fixed procedures (Angelo and Cross 1993), and each CAT is designed to be as flexible as possible so that faculty can adapt them to their own particular needs. Therefore, faculty should be encouraged to use only what works best for them.

Feedback on Classroom Assessment

Angelo and Cross's model has indeed made an impact on the discussion of improving college instruction, and references to the CATs have permeated the literature. The model has been called "promising and dynamic," offering opportunities "to refine instructional objectives, teaching methods, or evaluation techniques quickly" (Johnson, McCormick, Prus, and Rogers 1993, p. 160). The model not only helps faculty to measure students' learning; by involving students positively in the instructional process, Classroom Assessment can actually become an active learning technique (Meyers and Jones 1993; Sorcinelli 1994). The model has three strong advantages: faculty are influenced most by research they conduct; research strategies are flexible and involve small samples in actual settings; and the focus of the model on improving instruction based on research appeals to faculty (Boice 1992). The most significant aspect of the model, however, is the ease with which faculty can successfully use it (Boice 1992).

After pursuing campuswide implementations of Classroom Assessment, several institutions report that "classrooms are more charged with the energy of learning [and] students are more involved in their learning than ever before" (Obler, Slark, and Umbdenstock 1993, p. 218). "What is evident in all the projects is an increased collegewide emphasis on teaching and learning that has generated faculty revitalization" (p. 221). Faculty enthusiasm for the CATs has been noted at comprehensive universities (Berry, Filbeck, Rothstein-Fisch, and Saltman 1991) and community colleges alike (Stetson 1991). The CATs are "excellent examples of ways teachers can experiment in their own classrooms" (Centra 1993, pp. 113–14), and several CATs have been described as simple to use and helpful in the feedback they provide (Davis 1993).

Faculty at the University of Rhode Island describe the model as useful, particularly because of the simple techniques requiring minimal effort that provide needed information (Erickson and Strommer 1991). The model is "compelling" and "a critical component of the instructional innovation process," and "in addition to its promise as a way to improve student learning, Classroom Assessment is significant as an approach to developing teaching expertise" (Nummedal 1994, pp. 302–4). Several benefits accrue from using the CATs, including students' heightened awareness of their own learning (in addition to increased knowledge of course content), greater cooperation in the classroom to assist learning, and increased faculty participation in learning about teaching (Kort 1992). The Classroom Assessment model is a "quick and easy but very useful research approach" (Lucas 1994, p. 112).

The process of using the CATs as a research agenda by faculty has been praised as an opportunity to gain insight (McKeachie 1994). Even if "a systematic study" is not conducted, faculty can find "helpful ideas" by using the techniques (p. 339). The model "has been particularly helpful to teachers trying to understand their students" (Brookfield 1995, p. 94) and "is popular with faculty attempting to assess their teaching strengths and weaknesses" (Meyers and Jones 1993, p. 16). "Faculty across the country have engaged in the activity," and "much better teaching and learning has come about as a consequence of the classroom research/assessment movement" (Weimer 1996, p. 9).

The Classroom Assessment model clearly has created a wide and enthusiastic audience. In terms of its simplicity to implement and to adapt by individual faculty members and its potential value to both faculty and students, the model may indeed be one of the most powerful instructional development tools yet developed. The model is empowering for students as well as faculty, and one of its certain benefits may be its capability to unite everyone in the education process to enhance learning.

Other Forms of Assessment

In addition to the four models already discussed, individual college faculty can apply several other techniques for self-assessment, including the Cognitive Interaction Analysis System, quality circles, Four-Phase Feedback, the Episode of Teaching Growth, and evaluation data. These techniques also help to provide useful data to the instructor who wishes to improve teaching. Because these techniques do not fit within the definition of models for this report, they are only briefly described here.

Cognitive Interaction Analysis System

An approach to assessment by faculty that focuses on the communication taking place in the classroom, the Cognitive Interaction Analysis System (CIAS) uses coded data on classroom verbal interaction to help the instructor develop conclusions about the teaching and learning taking place. Developed by Johnson (1976, 1978) and based on the work of Flanders (1970), CIAS uses 10 categories for assessing classroom communication. Seven of the categories involve spoken communication from the teacher: acceptance of students' attitudes, positive reinforcement, value-free feedback, questions, lecture, instructions, and criticism. Students' responses are categorized as cognitive and noncognitive; the final category is silence. The technique includes procedures for recording these utterances as well as matrices for analyzing the recorded interactions. Because of the complexity of managing the recorded data on matrices, a computer program has been developed to help facilitate its analysis (Johnson 1978).

Quality circles

Originally developed as a procedure for continuous improvement in industry, the quality circle is basically an exercise to involve all participants in the process of decision making (Crocker, Chiu, and Charney 1984). The technique has also been applied to education, particularly for the enhancement of administrative operations (Kahn and Simmons 1990; Romine 1981). For individual faculty members, quality circles can be applied within the classroom, offering students and faculty the opportunity to exchange relevant information about specific experiences in the classroom (Hirshfield 1984; Kogut 1984; Weimer 1990). In terms of gathering information from students, this approach may appear to be an extension of the Classroom Assessment model. But instead of collecting individual written comments from students, the instructor would use the quality circle to receive immediate small-group feedback. The loss of anonymity in this case could, however, limit feedback if quiet students withhold their input or the group influences the tone of the discussion.

As a technique for developing classroom procedures and decisions, the quality circle has the potential to succeed, similar to that in industry. Students can provide helpful insight for making decisions, and their involvement in the process can make students feel more responsible for their learning. In fact, students' participation in disciplinary decision making has become a powerful motivating incentive for positive student behavior, even among younger groups (Glasser 1990).

Four-Phase Feedback

A procedure similar to Weimer's Five-Step Process for Improving Teaching, Four-Phase Feedback is described as a procedure for collecting feedback and applying it to the process of improving teaching and learning (Menges and Rando 1996). The four phases of the process include "(1) seeing and gathering, (2) interpreting and valuing, (3) planning and building, and (4) doing and checking" (pp. 233–34). The first phase involves a recognition of a problem and the search for information to solve the problem. Once the information is obtained, it must be evaluated for accuracy and usefulness in phase two. Designing a plan of action follows in the third phase, and the fourth phase includes implementation and evaluation of the plan. Like Weimer's model and most problem-solving procedures, Four-Phase Feedback incorporates the basic steps related to preparing, implementing, and evaluating a plan for change.

Episode of Teaching Growth

One more assessment technique comprising four stages represents the perceived growth process of college faculty. Incorporating a situation, faculty's reaction to it, information gathering, and the faculty member's reflection, the Episode of Teaching Growth describes how faculty learn from their experiences in the classroom (Chism 1993). Because the technique also resembles a learning process, faculty might not always be aware of these stages during the course of their careers. Typically, faculty react to a particular instructional problem and receive feedback on the consequences of the action taken. As faculty reflect on this feedback, they may develop insight into the wisdom of the action taken or realize that a different action would have been preferable. Faculty can use this technique to assess their behavior in the classroom and their problem-solving procedures.

Evaluation data

Faculty evaluation programs typically provide assessment information specific to individual instructors for the purpose of summative personnel decisions. Hence, summative evaluation data, unlike formative data, usually are not helpful for improving instruction. Nonetheless, a faculty evaluation can provide important feedback for the faculty member. For example, students' comments on faculty rating forms at the end of a semester could indicate some problems with the text that can prompt the faculty member to select another one. A colleague's recommendation that a faculty member's syllabus, especially the supplemental bibliography, needs to be revised could also affect instruction.

The teaching portfolio is one aspect of a faculty evaluation program that can be the source of particularly useful feedback.* Although portfolios are commonly used for summative evaluation, the personal development of portfolios by individual faculty members contributes to faculty reflection on the teaching process. Depending on the intended use of the portfolio, items to be included could be examples of a faculty member's significant achievements (Edgerton, Hutchings, and Quinlan 1991) or reflective narratives about one's typical instructional practice (Seldin 1991). Faculty intent on improving the effectiveness of their teaching can use the collection of data for the portfolio as a search for meaningful and useful feedback. The teaching portfolio, like many of the other techniques and models in this section, is a relatively recent development, yet its application, although

---

*See Murray *Forthcoming* for a definitive discussion of the teaching portfolio.

certainly not yet universal in American higher education, is flourishing (Braskamp and Ory 1994; Murray 1995; Zubizarreta 1995).

DISCUSSION/SHARING MODELS

Faculty are the major contributors to change in the class-room; hence, the most direct source of current classroom innovations should be faculty members themselves. Because faculty are inclined to accept only those changes that they deem necessary or desirable, supervisory coercion or even dissemination of innovations tends to be unsuccessful (Gaff 1978; Turner and Boice 1986; Weimer 1990). In general, faculty tend to get new ideas for the classroom more readily from their colleagues (Quinn 1994). If faculty are both the preferred developers and dispensers of innovations in the classroom, then techniques to facilitate their sharing should enhance the improvement of teaching and learning.

The key, of course, is to conceive of a method to bring faculty together to facilitate this kind of sharing. For the models described in this section, the typical isolation of faculty as a result of the classroom structure is a liability that must be overcome. Thus, the two models selected for discussion in this section have particular aspects that can induce faculty to share with their colleagues. One model is designed for faculty control of time and agenda. The other offers faculty a flexible opportunity to meet with colleagues in their own discipline. Hence, these models for generating faculty sharing can address some personal faculty needs as well as infuse strategies for improvement into the classroom.

Great Teachers Seminar

In 1969, Roger Garrison hosted an experimental faculty development seminar in Maine that became the inspiration for the development of an extraordinary concept for faculty discussion and collaboration. One of the participants at that event was David Gottshall, who a year later developed, with Garrison's blessing, the Illinois Great Teachers Seminar. By 1978, Gottshall's annual event had become the National Great Teachers Seminar. Like Gottshall, some of the partici-pants from other regions of the country adopted the move-ment's major features and founded their own regional ver-sions of the seminar: the Iowa Great Teachers Workshop at Lake Okoboji, the Pacific Northwest Great Teachers Seminar, and the Texas Great Teacher Roundup (Gottshall 1993).

Now over 25 years old and international in scope, the Great Teachers movement has indeed become a popular and influential aspect of college teaching. Originally designed for two-year college faculty (because two-year colleges are

devoted primarily to teaching and learning rather than research), the basic principles of the Great Teachers Seminar
(GTS) have been applied to other groups of faculty intent on
instructional development. Essentially, the GTS is a flexible,
process-oriented workshop, with faculty as the major resource, to facilitate the exchange of information. Its "focus is
not on the teaching of specific disciplines, but rather on the
art of teaching" (Gottshall 1993, p. 1).

The GTS was developed around five essential purposes:
the recognition of good teaching, the search for instructional
ideas not bound by disciplines, the nourishment of reflection
and self-assessment, the process of instructional problem solving, and the promotion of faculty sharing and collaboration
(Gottshall 1993; Reinhard and Layng 1994). Relying on an
acknowledgment of the principles of change theory (Hord,
Rutherford, Huling-Austin, and Hall 1987), the GTS is a visible
example of the dynamic qualities inherent in faculty-driven
faculty development. Moreover, each seminar is distinctive.
The GTS is "a continuing adventure in staff development"
(Gottshall 1993, p. 14).

Four basic presumptions
The basis for the GTS exists in four explicit, logical suppositions. First, as suggested earlier, faculty tend to be more
receptive to instructional input from other faculty. "Properly
facilitated shop talk can be the highest form of staff development" (Gottshall 1993, p. 7). Second, the fundamental diversity of faculty from different disciplines, representing varying
interests and experiences, supports instructional ingenuity.
Third, the essential resource of a group of faculty is the collective capability they generate as a whole. This resulting
synergy exceeds the capabilities of any single specialist in
college teaching. Fourth, to teach well is to simplify. In other
words, less input delivers more results (Boice 1992; Gottshall 1993).

Necessary characteristics
The key to the success of the GTS is partially its list of defining aspects. These conditions tend to differentiate the genuine GTS from any other meeting or conference. Unlike
typical gatherings of educators, the GTS should not have a
preplanned agenda. Although potentially troubling for some
faculty and possibly alarming to administrators, the flexible

last-minute agenda that results from participants' input generates benefits that far outweigh any of the imaginable drawbacks of abandoning traditional planning procedures. The normal GTS agenda is extracted from two short essays—describing a successful instructional idea and a troublesome classroom dilemma—written by participating faculty before the event. Accordingly, the director and the facilitators of the event do not contribute their own views to the agenda (Gottshall 1993).

Because the content of the event is not established before the seminar begins, the preparation of a schedule in advance is also precluded. Schedules lack flexibility (Gottshall 1993), and the establishment of a schedule requires that it be observed to demonstrate command of the situation. Unfortunately, the rigidity inherent in a schedule eliminates opportunities to consider new ideas or adjust the timing for those that require more or less time. The GTS instead relies on a list of activities prepared a few hours in advance.

Good teaching involves a certain amount of contemplation, which is also a necessary part of any learning activity.

Often meetings of educators include a keynote speaker or facilitator considered an expert in the field, from whom participants will glean a vast array of insight. The GTS is fundamentally devoid of such hired guns, however. The inherent philosophy of the GTS is the greater benefit accrued from pooling the capabilities and knowledge of professionals whose daily experience is in the classroom. The characteristic strength of this synergy is also one of the major concepts conveyed to participants in a typical GTS.

Faculty, who are thus given an opportunity to share their ideas and experiences, may also be inclined to share their gripes. Hence, the seminar begins with a consensus of all participants to focus their entire seminar experience on pragmatic and supportive efforts. The premise for this caveat is that negative discussions, an all-too-frequent element in faculty lounges, do not accomplish favorable results. "There is no room for bad news; only good news is acceptable" (Gottshall 1993, p. 11). After all, the most important rewards participants receive are useful ideas. Moreover, everyone accepts the mutual participation common to the small-group teaching method. No "stars," "clowns," or "wallflowers" are allowed. The operative word in this seminar is "sharing."

Good teaching involves a certain amount of contemplation, which is also a necessary part of any learning activity. One weakness displayed by poor lecturers is the delivery of a lecture that leaves no time in the middle for thought. Thus, the GTS necessarily includes ample opportunities for reflection, much like any good lecture should. Again, this particular element of the seminar may disturb the administrator who has become distanced from the classroom. But "free" time for reflective thought is an extremely important component of good teaching. With the allowance of sufficient unscheduled time, participants can begin to assign their own meanings to the numerous ideas and concepts discussed.

One of the two basic segments of the seminar is problem solving, and participants can expect to occupy much of their time dealing with the difficulties presented in the initial essays. Care must be taken with this process, however. People who allow a problem to become too complicated will make it more difficult to solve. Similarly, a problem that is made simple has a simple solution. For example, a faculty member concerned about students' cheating on tests decided to construct several different forms of each test. Unfortunately, the problem was made worse because the teacher did not have time to make so many different tests, distributing the tests in class was cumbersome, and grading them was a nightmare—leading to the conclusion that less is more (Gottshall 1993, p. 11).

While these important guidelines for a GTS that is true to its original intentions imply a certain rigidity in the process, the all-important flexibility of the event results from the diversity of the participants. Thus, the seminars appear to resemble one another, yet the content and the outcomes are always different. And without these necessary ingredients, the event would not be a GTS (Gottshall 1993).

The continuing adventure

The GTS has demonstrated its appeal around the country. In addition to the three descendants of the original Illinois Great Teachers Seminar in Iowa, Oregon, and Texas, Gottshall established seminars in California, Hawaii, Arizona, British Columbia, Connecticut, Missouri, North Carolina, North Dakota, Ohio, Ontario, Utah, and West Virginia, and some of these events have also led to individual college seminars. For example, over 50 such events have been conducted just in California. A survey of 100 community colleges indicates the "relatively common practice" of seminars by 'great teachers'" (Lauridsen 1994, p. 240).

The seminars themselves seem to be the chief means for disseminating the GTS model, as published accounts of Garrison's and Gottshall's work have been minimal (Garrison 1969; Gottshall 1993; Reinhard and Layng 1994) and reports of the model's effectiveness seem not to exist. Thus, the popularity of the GTS appears to be the only analysis available. Based on the faculty's resistance to efforts to improve teaching (Gaff 1978; Turner and Boice 1986; Weimer 1990), however, the well-established success of the model may be a sufficient recommendation.

Academic Alliances

Another initiative to bring faculty together for professional discussion and sharing of ideas began in 1981 with a project called Strengthening the Humanities through Foreign Language and Literature Studies. The concept was centered around the goal of establishing a community of scholars within specific disciplines to focus on quality instruction, much like county medical or legal organizations have worked for quality in their respective professions. The initial project, funded by grants from the National Endowment for the Humanities, the Rockefeller Foundation, the MacArthur Foundation, and the Exxon Education Foundation, became known as Academic Alliances: School/College Faculty Collaboratives (Gaudiani 1985; Gaudiani, Krug, and Slaughter 1984).

Like the GTS, the Academic Alliance model focuses on faculty sharing. By 1985, over 100 Academic Alliances in 40 states were established in foreign languages, English, history, biology, chemistry, and physics (Gaudiani 1985). The alliances are intended to concentrate on the needs of faculty in a single subject field at all levels, kindergarten through university, within a local geographic area. Often operating in concert with state and regional disciplinary associations, the alliances, which typically range from 15 to 50 faculty, meet frequently (monthly or bimonthly) and can thus serve as a bridge to the larger group. As travel budgets continue to be reduced, this concept of a local professional group can truly benefit those who are unable to attend national, regional, or even state meetings.

The Academic Alliances model operates on five basic premises developed by Maeroff (1983) that are indicative of successful partnerships (Gaudiani and Burnett 1986). Logically, these premises resemble the concepts that support the

GTS. First, individuals involved in such collaborative efforts must understand that they have something to communicate. Second, participants should abandon any real or perceived notions of personal position or standing. Hence, individual reputation within a discipline and a teacher's grade-level assignment are not considered in the interest of establishing and maintaining a cooperative environment. This goal can be achieved by focusing on the third premise, placing the problem(s) to be solved at the forefront of the endeavor. Fourth, some kind of incentive will also further collaboration. Finally, the project's success can be further enhanced by emphasizing the role of the partnership rather than its structure. Thus, the various alliances are provided with some guidance to accomplish their goals (Gaudiani and Burnett 1986).

Purpose of the alliances

Clearly, the establishment of a perpetual collaborative of local faculty at all levels is the major objective of the alliances, and this goal is not unlike the expectation of continuous collaboration as a result of the Great Teachers Seminar. The alliances also are intended to keep the applicable discipline's faculty current in the field and to shoulder the obligation for excellence in the profession without excessive expenditures of time and money. "The Academic Alliance project is built on the assumption that teachers, working collectively, can be a powerful and cost-effective force in improving the quality of their own professional lives" (Gaudiani 1985, p. 70).

Moreover, the collaborative groups can be an effective catalyst to break down the isolation inherent in teaching. Along the same lines, participating faculty are expected to foster mutual understanding by setting aside intolerance of one another and building shared esteem for colleagues. Hence, meetings of the alliance, like those of the GTS, can help to create a sense of harmony and cooperation among faculty. These efforts are intended to improve education through the development of faculty, who are indeed the most valuable resource in education (Gaudiani, Krug, and Slaughter 1984).

Typical alliance meetings

Resembling the GTS, the model for Academic Alliances involves meetings for faculty conducted by faculty (Gaudiani, Krug, and Slaughter 1984). Institutions do not form partnerships as part of an alliance (Gaudiani and Burnett 1986). Each meeting is designed around literature or conference reviews, instructional demonstrations or exchanges, or panel discussions (Gaudiani 1985). Much like a conference with concurrent sessions, these discussions and demonstrations can be scheduled simultaneously to meet participants' various needs. Whether the group's need is to maintain an up-to-date approach to instruction or simply to share successful practices, the typical meeting format can be designed appropriately, like that for the GTS. Lengthy presentations are to be avoided. The management of alliance meetings is also similar to the GTS: No single group or individual controls the process, and "expert" speakers generally are not involved.

Funding such events is relatively simple as a result of the limited needs for most meetings. Keeping the group within the local area precludes the need for travel and lodging expenditures. And because the meetings are usually limited to a few hours and existing rent-free space is often adequate, additional costs can be eliminated as well. Moreover, an allowance for guest speaker or facilitator fees is unnecessary (Gaudiani 1985).

Alliances uniting faculty

The Academic Alliances model is another example of dissemination that has been achieved primarily without published reports. The limited coverage of the model in the literature is primarily the result of the initial project's administrative office (Siegal 1985; Silber and Moore 1989; Watkins 1989). Nevertheless, the concept has been adopted across the country, with over 200 alliances established in fewer than 10 years.

With a MacArthur Foundation grant, the American Association for Higher Education assumed major support of the project in 1988 (Gaudiani 1990). The Academic Alliances project continued under the guidance of AAHE until 1992, when it was determined the model no longer needed national support to continue. The operation of the alliances naturally devolved to local institutions. Since then, variations of the model have also been developed, for example, the Discipline Dialogues project of the Maricopa Community Colleges (Travis 1992).

Although a formal evaluation of the model was planned for 1986 (Gaudiani 1985), no comprehensive study examining the overall impact of the alliances was conducted. Individual alliance groups have, however, felt a strong sense of accomplishment, particularly in improved self-esteem and the professional attitude of participating faculty (Gaudiani 1985). Even administrators were impressed with the results of the project.

After AAHE took over management of the project, several case studies were performed to measure faculty members' response to the model.* The collective reaction from faculty during these case studies indicated that they considered the Academic Alliances a worthwhile activity. The model's inherent informality appeared to have fostered more effective programs, and the concept of faculty members' designing and conducting activities for their professional development has become attractive to college and university faculty. This faculty-driven process can also serve as an incentive for greater faculty participation in development programs.

Related Techniques
Two additional approaches for encouraging sharing among faculty—consultation/collaboration and teaching academies —are described only briefly. Neither is as well-defined as the Great Teachers Seminar or Academic Alliances, and both have numerous possible variations. Further, neither technique fits the definition of a model for this report.

Consultation/collaboration
Faculty are not restricted to special occasions, such as the GTS and Academic Alliances, for sharing with their colleagues. Informal consulting or collaborating with fellow faculty members, while relatively new as a faculty development technique, is yet another approach that is becoming increasingly accepted in higher education (Austin and Baldwin 1991; Baldwin and Austin 1995). Collaboration among faculty peers can also be applied to an assessment process (Aleamoni 1987; Heppner and Johnston 1994; Keig and Waggoner 1994). A faculty mentor program is yet another application of this collaborative arrangement (Boice 1992; Sorcinelli 1995).

The resemblance of this technique to peer teaching or cooperative learning, although applicable strictly to faculty in

_____
*Lou Albert 1996, personal communication.

this case, should be apparent (Johnson, Johnson, and Smith 1991; Whitman 1988). While formal consultation has become a common form of faculty development on many campuses (Annis 1989; Lewis 1988; Nyquist 1986), such an application of professional consultation is not an aspect of this particular technique, which involves only peer consultants rather than professional faculty developers. Each of these forms of collaboration and consultation may appear to be distinct, yet they all share a familiar principle that connects them: faculty links as "a matter of social support" (Boice 1992, p. 129). Essentially, the technique in its many forms involves the practice of faculty working together to learn, to solve problems, or to create (Brinko 1991; Carroll and Pattishall 1986; Ferren and Geller 1983). Hence, the common thread of faculty helping faculty runs through this section.

Teaching academies

Connected to some institutional efforts to recognize and reward faculty, the concept of the teaching academy is intended to both recognize excellent teaching and to promote sharing among academy members and the institution's faculty (Chism, Fraser, and Arnold 1996). The academies vary in their individual objectives, fiscal support, functions, relationship to the rest of the institution, organizational form, and selection of members, and they have varied goals:

- *To advocate the importance of teaching*
- *To create an appropriate reward structure for teaching*
- *To promote a sense of community among teachers*
- *To serve as role models*
- *To foster research on college teaching and learning*
- *To advise the institution on teaching policies and practices* (Chism, Fraser, and Arnold 1996, p. 27).

These academies have been designed at such institutions as Ohio State University, Thomas Jefferson University, the University of Arkansas, and the University of Wisconsin.

Institutions as well as faculty receive benefits from these programs (Chism, Fraser, and Arnold 1996). The commitment to teaching and its effectiveness has an impact on the institution, while the sharing among faculty that can lead to the development of a community of scholars benefits both faculty and the institution. The academies are a source of

Connected to some institutional efforts to recognize and reward faculty, the concept of the teaching academy is intended to both recognize excellent teaching and to promote sharing among academy members and the institution's faculty.

incentives for improving one's teaching. Nevertheless, the academies also have some disadvantages, among them the resulting increase in workload that generally is demanded of academy members and the reduction in actual teaching assignments for academy members, which causes the institutions to lose valuable teaching expertise. In general, however, the advantages are greater than the disadvantages for the institutions that implement academies (Chism, Fraser, and Arnold 1996).

DISSEMINATION MODELS

The sharing of innovative ideas among professionals is certainly one effective approach to foster institutionwide improvement. Unfortunately, a seminar or alliance may not be conveniently available, and the sharing possible through collaborative efforts understandably is limited. Some faculty may not have the opportunity to learn from the institution's most creative or most adventurous innovators. Others may not feel the desire or need to share or learn from colleagues. Additional opportunities to distribute functional ideas are a necessary complement to the faculty sharing models. These dissemination techniques are often provided as an element of institutional support for individual faculty development.

Centers for Improving Teaching

Although many college faculty development programs can serve as a somewhat limited source of ideas for improving teaching and learning, the pursuit of existing research to augment a program's collection of innovations may be beyond the capabilities of an individual college's efforts. Northwestern University developed a model program designed to accomplish both development and dissemination, in part through the efforts of Benjamin Bloom. The Center for the Improvement of Teaching and Learning was established at the City Colleges of Chicago as a national resource for information on instructional practice (Guskey 1988; Guskey, Barshis, and Easton 1982).

The center's distinctive approach

While its essential purpose was instructional research, the center was committed to efforts that transcended most research centers. All the center's work had to result in pragmatic applications to college classrooms. The focus of the research, therefore, included the techniques and differences of both teaching and learning (Guskey, Barshis, and Easton 1982). Further, each practical idea also had to demonstrate an exceptional impact on student learning with comparatively minor efforts in instructional manipulation, a so-called "multiplier effect" (Guskey 1988; Guskey, Barshis, and Easton 1982). The center's efforts were based on the assumptions that the improvement of instruction was possible on a grand scale and that faculty could generally advance to the capabilities of master teachers.

The center's efforts were based on the assumptions that the improvement of instruction was possible on a grand scale and that faculty could generally advance to the capabilities of master teachers.

The center's projects were drawn from three primary sources: educational literature, working faculty, and eminent scholars. Searching for the techniques and differences that have demonstrated a sizable impact on teaching and/or learning, the center's staff conducted thorough literature reviews and collected and analyzed effective techniques suggested by faculty from around the country. The center even maintained researchers on its staff who were recognized experts in the areas of teaching and learning in higher education. With additional recommendations from these authorities in the field, the center was able to profit from a range of potentially innovative ideas.

The concepts generated by all three sources were then transformed into procedures or techniques to be applied at only one or two colleges in pilot programs. The pilot projects that demonstrated particular promise could then be expanded into demonstration projects for up to six locations. If these advanced projects proved educationally effective and fiscally efficient, the center could then disseminate its findings through meetings and publications. The anticipated outcomes of these projects were expected to enhance the vitality of the faculty, motivating them through the development of an environment that encourages experimentation (Guskey, Barshis, and Easton 1982). Although results of the center's early studies were not entirely favorable, "the vast majority produced *exceptionally* positive results" (Guskey 1988, p. 9).

Spread of the concept

In essence, the Center for the Improvement of Teaching and Learning was a new creation. While most improvement centers focused on the development of faculty (Gaff 1975; Group for Human Development 1974), this new model served as a hybrid for faculty growth, development of resources, and research in teaching. This center model has not been widely implemented, as the requirements and institutional resources of specific colleges and universities may proscribe the establishment of such a center on their campuses. Consequently, the development of the center's model in the literature is limited as well.

Even so, other similar centers have been developed. Since the opening of the center at the City Colleges of Chicago, Lord Fairfax Community College in Virginia (McMullen 1982), the University of Washington (Nyquist 1986), and the

University of Colorado–Boulder (Shea 1990) all established comparable centers. Similarly, other institutions—the University of Texas–Austin, Ball State University, Ohio State University, the University of Toronto, and Harvard University, among others—seem to have adopted the model for their own particular needs (Gullette 1984; Wadsworth 1988). Perhaps the unusual nature and the requirements for establishing such a center for instructional improvement will affect the potential for further expansion of the model's use.

Publications

Both national and local faculty development programs have produced a wide range of published resources on teaching, including journals, newsletters, and books. Several notable examples have been designed for the dissemination of ideas and innovations for improving teaching and learning: the Jossey-Bass series, New Directions for Teaching and Learning, launched in 1980; three journals, *College Teaching, Journal on Excellence in College Teaching,* and *Innovative Higher Education;* McKeachie's *Teaching Tips* (1994), now in its ninth edition; the Sage series, Survival Skills for Scholars; the contribution to the ASHE Reader Series, *Teaching and Learning in the College Classroom* (Feldman and Paulsen 1994); and the series published by the Professional and Organizational Development Network in Higher Education, *To Improve the Academy.* Three publications in particular appear to stand out as especially useful to individual faculty: *Innovation Abstracts, The Teaching Professor,* and *The National Teaching and Learning Forum.*

Reading is the second most common activity by which faculty gather new ideas for teaching (Quinn 1994). Yet most faculty do not seem to have much time to read about teaching. In fact, many faculty members tend to place less significance on reading for teaching improvement (Weimer 1988). Instructors often collect large amounts of useful and important reading material—which finds a familiar home on the corners of faculty desks (Quinn 1994). Add to this dilemma of growing stacks of necessary reading matter the modern phenomenon of the enormous increase in information. The thought of keeping up with useful, or even important, reading has become a more unrealistic dream.

Consequently, faculty who may be inclined to scan the literature for ideas about teaching and learning require concise resources that will not place another burden on their already limited time. Because the bulk of faculty reading that focuses on teaching is also relatively casual (Quinn 1994), publications in the format of a newsletter may be especially useful. The three publications described in the following paragraphs fit this definition and offer busy faculty substance without excessive space.

Innovation Abstracts

A creation of the National Institute for Staff and Organizational Development (NISOD), based at the University of Texas in Austin, *Innovation Abstracts* has been published weekly during the school year since 1979. The publication normally covers the front and back of a single page, with one or more brief articles written primarily by college faculty. The focus of each article is a successful technique or innovation and its application by the author or an idea for improving instruction. Each contributor's address is included at the end of each article to provide a point of reference for further discussion and questions. The series was referenced by the ERIC system beginning with Volume 3 (Watkins 1981). Although the overall mission of NISOD is targeted toward two-year colleges, the messages found among the issues of *Innovation Abstracts* can apply in classrooms at all levels of higher education.

The Teaching Professor

A similar, brief periodical, with more representation among its authors from four-year colleges and universities, *The Teaching Professor* has been published monthly during the school year since 1987 by Magna Publications (see Weimer 1987 for an early example). Although this periodical is generally more lengthy than *Innovation Abstracts,* the average length of articles in both publications is comparable, again a strong advantage for faculty. Like the NISOD publication, *The Teaching Professor* focuses on ideas and innovations that can improve and bring new life to teaching and learning. The purpose of these contributions, as the publisher has stated, is to help faculty resist the temptation to continue using worn-out lecture notes and equally worn-out teaching methods.

The National Teaching and Learning Forum

The George Washington University, in conjunction with James Rhem and Associates and the ERIC Clearinghouse on Higher Education, initiated yet another type of newsletter, also written by educators, in 1991. Oryx Press has since taken over publication of this newsletter. Because of the faculty contributions to *The National Teaching and Learning Forum,* this publication offers practical advice, much like *Innovation Abstracts* and *The Teaching Professor.* The articles offer a variety of case studies, tested classroom techniques, and applications of research in teaching and learning in a conversational format that endeavors to speak to faculty in all subject fields. With six issues published during the academic year, *The National Teaching and Learning Forum* provides more substance than the other two periodicals, usually incorporating five or more articles per issue. This publication recently added an on-line edition.

Three advantages help to make these publications stand out as an effective dissemination model for improving college teaching. First and most important, faculty, drawing on their direct classroom experience for their ideas, contribute most of the articles. Second, the ability of the contributors to deliver their messages concisely and completely is a tremendous benefit for busy faculty members. Although an individual institution's faculty development newsletter can supply each of these two qualities, it usually cannot supply the range of contributions from across the nation.

These three publications are very similar, with the only major differences among them their length and typical contributors. Each publication should be equally useful to practicing faculty, although the major drawback to their usefulness is, of course, that they fit within the category of reading material. Because a sizable amount of obligatory reading material often exists, optional items, such as these brief publications, might not be widely read or the ideas contained in them often used. Consequently, the discussion models described in the previous section could be used to augment the dissemination of innovative classroom techniques contained in the newsletters. For example, individual faculty, each reading a selected article, can summarize the reading for discussion groups. Instructors who have already tried a

With six issues published during the academic year, The National Teaching and Learning Forum provides more substance than the other two periodicals, usually incorporating five or more articles per issue.

particular idea in the classroom can offer valuable examples in these discussions.

Although faculty exposed to these publications are generally extremely complimentary of each one, no formal evaluation of them appears to have been conducted. *The Teaching Professor* has been called "a runaway best seller" (Chism 1991, p. 237), but other references to these publications in the literature are rare. Current circulation figures can serve as a good indication of each publication's impact on the profession. *Innovation Abstracts* reported a circulation in excess of 75,000 in 1996; circulation figures for *The Teaching Professor* and *The National Teaching and Learning Forum* were 20,000 and 3,000, respectively. *The National Teaching and Learning Forum* recently expanded its circulation, including international subscriptions, with its on-line edition.*

---

*Addresses for these publications are listed in Appendix B.

CLINICAL DEVELOPMENT MODELS

College and university faculty usually are not adequately prepared to teach. Faculty require a knowledge of various teaching methods and sufficient experience using these methods to develop their teaching skills. For those who need to develop these skills, the chance to learn and experiment within a supportive clinical environment could be desirable. This section describes a model that provides such a nonthreatening opportunity for development. Because of the model's format and clinical nature, faculty participants necessarily require some time away from their normal responsibilities. The essential clinical environment must be provided as well. Consequently, the cost of providing this developmental model to faculty can be significant.

Instructional Skills Workshop

An intensive pedagogical workshop that uses a clinical supervision context, the Instructional Skills Workshop (ISW) is intended to provide for college faculty what their public school counterparts generally experience—microteaching laboratory classes.

> *Microteaching is a scaled-down teaching encounter in which (typically) a teacher plans and teaches a lesson incorporating a behaviorally defined teaching skill, receives peer and video feedback, and reteaches the lesson. Thus, teachers experience practice with feedback and learn to discriminate effective from ineffective teaching behaviors* (Levinson-Rose and Menges 1981, p. 414).

Administered by college faculty for college faculty, the ISW offers this approach to microteaching as a nonthreatening, formative development activity. Developed in 1979 for the British Columbia Ministry of Education, the ISW was designed to meet the needs of college faculty who had little or no pedagogical training (Morrison 1985).

Components of the ISW

Essentially, the ISW is a complete package of opportunities for clinical development. Incorporated in the program are three separate stages of learning, with each successive level building on the development that participants gain in the previous session or sessions.

The basic instructional skills program. The primary element of preparation emphasizes the development of instructional skills. During this phase, faculty participants are involved in a rigorous four-day workshop designed to provide instruction and guided practice in pedagogy. Each workshop includes four to eight faculty participants and two trained faculty facilitators. This process focuses on the development of lesson plans, including instructional objective writing, and the presentation of short lessons (Morrison 1985). Thus, participating faculty have an opportunity to practice with existing instructional skills and experiment with new ones. It is important to note, however, that "the workshop does not presuppose a 'right way' to teach or learn" (Kort 1992, p. 66), and the workshop is not intended "to completely overhaul the instructor" (Bloor 1987, p. 2).

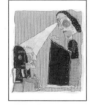

The basic ISW schedule comprises four six-hour days. The first day begins with the establishment of the positive, nonthreatening atmosphere necessary to the entire process. Also included in day one are a demonstration of both a minilesson and a feedback session, guidance in both giving and receiving feedback, and a lesson in instructional design skills. The remaining three days of the workshop are devoted to the presentations of minilessons and the performance of feedback sessions. Each participant is expected to provide a 10-minute minilesson during each of these three days' activities. The lessons are presented to the other participants, who serve as learners, while the instructor is videotaped (Bloor 1987). The use of videotape is a common technique for providing useful feedback to the instructor.

The minilessons are necessarily brief to limit the amount of feedback so that it is manageable for the instructor-participant. Because the minilessons must be limited to only 10 minutes, care must be taken to provide participant-learners with comprehensive coverage of only one concept that also does not require special prior instruction. Further, instructor-participants are expected to incorporate five key elements in each lesson: an introduction or "bridge-in," the lesson's objective, a pretest, active learning that involves experimenting with unfamiliar teaching styles, and a post-test (Bloor 1987).

Clearly, including all of these requirements in a mere 10-minute lesson is a tall order. The participants are therefore expected to spend a considerable amount of time preparing each lesson. The care taken to completely explain a concept and to make the entire presentation succinct may draw the participant's attention to the diligence required for each concept in actual instruction.

Each lesson is immediately followed by a 20-minute feedback period guided by the facilitators to ensure that the non-threatening atmosphere achieved on the first day is maintained. During the first seven minutes of the feedback session, participant-learners are asked to reflect on the learning experience in writing on guided forms. Facilitators then lead participant-learners in a discussion to share these experiences during the remainder of the feedback period. Throughout the process, the videotape can be used to illustrate pertinent comments (Bloor 1987).

Feedback sessions are generally guided by three fundamental questions relating to the actions that facilitated learning, those that interfered with learning, and those that could be incorporated to improve instruction. The intent of the workshop is to focus on the *process* of teaching the lesson, not to dwell on its content. The result, consequently, should lead instructor-participants to develop as professionals without losing the necessary confidence or feeling of self-worth.

Training facilitators. The second stage of the workshop is a training session for facilitators. The process of developing instructional skills can be understandably stressful and therefore requires the guidance of skilled facilitators. This Facilitator Skills Workshop is designed to prepare instructors experienced with the ISW to operate the workshop at their own colleges (Morrison 1985). This workshop can be conducted as part of an ISW, with the addition of a fifth day.

Preparation of trainers. For those who wish to further their experience with the ISW, a one-day session to instruct facilitator-trainers is the third stage of the model. This component of the workshop prepares the individual who has completed the training in facilitator skills and has led several ISWs to conduct the Facilitator Skills Workshop (Morrison 1985). Thus, the complete ISW package can be accomplished in six days of instruction. For institutions with time constraints that could prohibit the consecutive schedule, alternative formats on weekends or evenings are also possible (Bloor 1987; Morrison 1985).

The dissemination of instructional skills
The Instructional Skills Workshops were initially conducted by the British Columbia Ministry of Education for its provincial colleges (Morrison 1985). The first workshops were field tests involving both experienced and new faculty in liberal arts and occupational programs, who reacted to the ISW enthusiastically (Kort 1992). As the British Columbia Ministry of Education did not fund the workshops, "the number of workshop participants is one important measure of the value placed by institutions on the program" (Morrison 1985, p. 80). By 1985, almost 2,000 faculty members had attended these workshops, with a total of 2,500 by 1987 (Bloor 1987; Morrison 1985).

After "a decade of success in British Columbia," the model was introduced in 1986 to community college faculty in California (Kort 1989, p. 1). Comments from participating faculty and administrators indicate the value of the model:

> *I've been teaching for about 12 years, without any kind of formal instruction in methodology, and although I thought I was doing a reasonable job, there was a secret apprehension or fear. It turned out that my coparticipants were not in the least judgmental or critical. . . . I feel highly energized by the process. . . .*

> *It has really heightened an awareness of instructional technique and provided many of us with an excellent opportunity to sharpen skills. . . .*

> *Until I got into the ISW, most of my professional development was technical in nature. Now I am much more aware of teaching styles and learning styles. . . . I guess I am moving from being teacher-oriented to being a lot more student-oriented* (Morrison 1985, p. 80).

By 1992, Instructional Skills Workshops were being conducted on 50 American campuses, led by facilitators from their own personnel. The model has been introduced to state universities as well (Morrison 1985).

Another Model: Teaching the Technology of Teaching
Although clinical development opportunities for college faculty are not too common, the ISW is not necessarily the

sole clinical development model. Teaching the Technology of Teaching, while similar to the ISW, is not as well developed, and it appears to have been implemented on only one campus. Coverage in the literature is extremely limited as well.

An approach that focuses on efficient practice by emphasizing the characteristics of good teachers and effective approaches used to strengthen teaching and learning, this model was conceived by Shackelford and Henak (1987) at Ball State University. The model consists primarily of three seminars that address effective faculty characteristics, syllabus and lesson preparation, measuring and adapting to the diversity of learners, assessment, communication skills and techniques, interventions for improving instruction, developing retention in students, instructional media development and use, and planning professional development. The three seminars emphasize planning, instruction, and professional development. While the active involvement of participants and opportunities for the participants to videotape their own minilessons have been incorporated into the model, the focused effort common to the ISW is lacking in this example. Approximately 140 faculty members participated in the model's activities at Ball State University between 1988 and 1992.

TEACHING/LEARNING MODELS

Because many college and university faculty were not specifically prepared for college teaching before they began their careers, they may also lack an understanding of learning theory. Thus armed, the most thoughtful instructors could reflect on their own learning habits and apply their discoveries accordingly. Yet faculty also need to know how others learn (Dinham 1996; Eble 1988). As the research on multiple intelligences and learning styles has so aptly demonstrated, everyone does not learn the same way (Claxton and Murrell 1987; Claxton and Ralston 1978; Gardner 1993). Further, college students are much more diverse today than they were when most current faculty attended college (Dinham 1996). With different experiences, interests, and motivations, these students can easily confound a scholar unschooled in learning theory.

If faculty are to assist students in the learning process, they will need a basic understanding of learning theory and knowledge of how the theory can be applied to the classroom. The models in this section provide faculty with supplementary theoretical constructs they might have missed in the progress of their preparation to teach. Considering that approaches to understanding cognitive learning and the diversity of learning styles are rather recent developments, many faculty could benefit from exposure to one or more of these models that address some of the basic concepts of teaching and learning. Two of the models presented delve into the domain of cognitive learning; the others are related to theories of learning styles.

If faculty are to assist students in the learning process, they will need a basic understanding of learning theory and knowledge of how the theory can be applied to the classroom.

Cognitive Instructional Intervention

Understanding how people learn has been the goal of educational psychology since its inception. With the advent of Skinnerian behaviorism earlier in this century, some educational psychologists may have concluded that the answer had been discovered. Since then, however, newer concepts of learning theory have appeared. What differentiates the more recent developments from the rigid behavioral concepts is an assumption that human beings do not necessarily behave in predictable patterns, as the behaviorists would like to believe. Among these enlightening inquiries have been the studies of memory systems, cognitive learning, and metacognition. One example of a theoretical approach to

---

understanding the learning process is Anderson's (1976, 1983) Adaptive Control of Thought (ACT).

Adaptive Control of Thought

Although people do behave somewhat independently and perhaps may learn in different ways and for different reasons, some characteristics of learning appear to be consistent. From the perspective of the research conducted on human memory, learning requires the participation of two basic types of memory: short-term or working memory and long-term memory (Anderson 1983; Shavelson, Webb, and Burstein 1986; Weinstein and Meyer 1991). The working memory is the active processor, directing a person in every thought process or action selected. But the working memory has limited and only temporary storage capacity. Therefore, much of the behavior governed by the working memory relies upon information stored in long-term memory. Conversely, long-term memory is the repository for information without the capability to independently govern action or thought. And long-term memory cannot interact with the environment, which is part of the function of working memory. Thus, the two components of memory are necessary for most action and thought processes (Anderson 1983).

Within long-term storage are two specific types of memory with two particularly exclusive purposes: declarative memory, for the retention of nonbehavioral information, and procedural memory, containing the stored directions for any type of activity known to the respective individual (Anderson 1982, 1983). Fundamentally, all of these components of human memory function together to allow thought and behavioral processes to continue in a seemingly ceaseless fashion. For a person to learn, therefore, information must be processed by the working memory, whether its source is the environment or long-term memory, and then preserved in long-term memory. The complete sequence is necessary for learning to actually occur (Anderson 1983).

The entire arrangement is similar to the various components of a computer system. The working memory, with its limited storage capacity and direct connections to the environment allowing it to receive and send messages, resembles the central processing unit (CPU) in a computer system and its links to the environment through the keyboard, mouse, and monitor. Like the working memory, the computer's RAM (random-access memory) of the CPU has minimal—and temporary—storage capacity. Further, the CPU requires the input of applications, or programs, to carry out any computer functions. Without the CPU, however, the computer cannot conduct any of these operations. Similarly, computer disks, both floppies and the hard drive, resemble the storage capacity of long-term memory, vast but incapable of action without transferring, or downloading, the stored information into the CPU.

This theoretical explanation of the use of memory in the learning process is important, but to help students learn, a more pragmatic application of this learning model for the classroom may be needed. After all, a basic understanding of the operation of the human memory is probably not sufficient to automatically manipulate information from the working memory to the long-term memory. Some effective techniques that can be practiced like any skill should be invaluable. Applicable to the ACT model are five such techniques, three for recall knowledge and two for generalization knowledge (Wallen 1990). Related to the lower cognitive levels in Bloom's Taxonomy (1956), these two types of knowledge are the most basic stages of learning (see figure 3). Simple recall involves the retrieval of information from the long-term memory to the working memory. Fundamentally relying on a certain amount of recall, generalization knowledge also involves the storage and retrieval of data within perceived relationships.

FIGURE 3

BLOOM'S TAXONOMY OF EDUCATIONAL OBJECTIVES

Evaluation
Synthesis
Analysis
Application
Comprehension
Knowledge

Recall learning

To assist students in the development of recall, faculty can incorporate three different strategies: rehearsal, elaboration, and organization (Anderson and Bower 1973; Weinstein and

Mayer 1986; Weinstein and Meyer 1991). The simple but cumbersome rehearsal technique involves mere repetition of the information until it is securely anchored in long-term memory. Because the amount of rehearsal necessary to accomplish this task is relative, but not necessarily obvious, this approach is not overwhelmingly efficient.

The other two recall techniques rely on the more precise use of uncomplicated clues that serve as direct links to the stored information. Elaboration requires the association of the information to be learned with already existing knowledge, hence its common reference, "learning by association." Therefore, the target to be recalled is the association, rather than the less familiar new information. To continue with the computer analogy (which is, by the way, an example of elaboration), the use of visual clues, or icons, in much modern software allows for more facile and direct recollection of procedures than the more abstract keystroke commands tend to warrant.

The most intricate technique for acquiring recall knowledge, organization is also the best approach for retrieving complex information. By reconfiguring great amounts of data in various ways, the learner is more capable of managing the process of storing and remembering the target information. Once again, the learner focuses on a specific cue, in this case the pattern of organization, as a memory key. Although several types of organization may be selected, a visual or observable representation, such as mind mapping, is preferred (see also the strategies suggested in the next model, Training for Information Processing). Computer technology again provides an example with the arrangement of the keys on the computer keyboard.

Generalization learning

Two instructional techniques can be used for assisting in the development of generalization knowledge: direct instruction and the discovery strategy (Bruner 1966; Wallen 1990). Direct instruction incorporates a specific sequence of procedures involving two essential steps. First, the learner acquires the requisite recall knowledge of a model generalization, or example for applying the generalization knowledge. He or she does so by initially designing an appropriate model generalization, identifying its target information, and developing an assessment for recalling the model generalization and instruction for its recall using rehearsal, elaboration, or organization.

The model generalization typically includes a descriptive name, a rule for application, and examples and nonexamples of the applied rule.

Once the recall knowledge of a model generalization has been acquired, the student is asked to apply the model generalization to other, distinct situations. Each application task should be accompanied by guidance from the instructor to ensure that the student will reflect upon errors in thinking or recognize problems in explaining the decision process. The application tasks continue with additional examples and guidance until the employment of the model generalization is smooth and accurate.

An example of this strategy applies to learning the parts of speech. For instance, the descriptive name for one part of speech is "noun." Its rule for application refers to a person, place, thing, or idea. Examples could be "teacher," "school," "apple," and "knowledge"; some nonexamples could be "learn," "with," and "easy." Thus, the model generalization is ready for learning as recall knowledge. Once this information is known, other examples and nonexamples can be applied to this model generalization for practice.

The procedure for implementing the discovery strategy to acquire generalization knowledge is less structured. An objective generalization category is identified and characteristics of the category in the form of critical and irrelevant attributes then established. Doing so helps to define the parameters of the generalization. Finally, examples and nonexamples for these attributes are discovered. One way to implement this strategy could involve the identification and categorization of trees by the shape and structure of leaves. Once students identify the basic shapes, they can then apply actual examples to these generalization categories.

Acquainting students with these strategies for recall and generalization knowledge should help students in the development of study skills. Yet helping students to learn such study techniques is not adequate.

They must also know how to use them and under what conditions. . . . The instructional decisions and teaching methods that we select and implement profoundly affect students' knowledge about strategies and their use of them. By understanding how students use these strategies, instructors can become more alert to ways of fostering the development and use of strategies through course structures and activities (Weinstein and Meyer 1991, p. 21).

Consequently, an understanding of learning processes, these manipulative techniques, and ways that faculty can make them work for students is one way to facilitate learning.

The distinctive ACT

Based on reactions to Anderson's work, the ACT model certainly filled a void in cognitive psychology. "Anderson has made a serious contribution to cognitive science, one that is supported by considerable scholarship and calculated respect for the scientific method" (Lehnert 1984, p. 855). Anderson's work is important and highly intellectual, "a magnificent scientific work [that] . . . repays fully the effort of reading it" (Craig 1978, p. 446). With Anderson's important argument for differentiating between declarative and procedural knowledge, his model is "the best integrative theory of the system level of cognition that we now have, and it provides a model for how such integrative investigations of the mind can be done" (Black 1984, p. 854).

Human memory theory and its application to learning is certainly not limited in the research literature or found only in Anderson's work. The vast amount of content in these areas of educational psychology can appear to make the educator's task of understanding learning theory more arduous. With the ACT model, faculty have an opportunity to develop this understanding more easily. As faculty develop a better understanding of learning principles, the needs of our increasingly diverse student population are more likely to be met. And the strategies for putting the model to work in the classroom can provide faculty with more tools to help students learn (Anderson and Bower 1973; Wallen 1990; Weinstein and Mayer 1986).

Training for Information Processing

Techniques for organizing information can greatly facilitate the learning and recall of relevant data. The way information is delivered or recorded as it is received can be extremely influential in facilitating the speed of learning as well as the duration of retention (DuBois 1986). Drawn from the fundamental principles of cognitive learning theory is a model for the representation of information for both the sender or instructor and the receiver or student (DuBois *n.d.*; DuBois, Alverson, and Staley 1979).

Lectures, and the resulting notes students take, often follow a standard outline format, an organization of the information that can be inherently complex and disordered. DuBois referred to this type of organization as "a cluster format." In this organizational pattern, indications of structure and relationships are often ill-defined or entirely lacking. Applying the organization strategy described earlier, DuBois's model for presenting and recording information promotes the use of two other organizational formats: hierarchies and sequences. Hence, the model focuses on the structure used to organize the information given or received.

Hierarchies
Knowledge includes structure, function, operation, and examples, all of which make the use of the cluster type of organization frequently cumbersome (DuBois *n.d.*). If this rather complex array of information is organized according to recognizable categories in a horizontal construct, much like a family tree, the information is easier to manage and to learn. Such a technique resembles that of mind mapping, in which the learner plots related concepts in branching patterns that extend out from a central idea (Buzan 1989). Other similar designs are diagrammed sentences and vertical organizational charts. Such hierarchical arrangements help to emphasize visually the relationships and functions of the various components incorporated in the information to be learned (see figure 4 for an example of a hierarchy).

Sequences
The other type of design for structuring information in DuBois's model is the sequence. Instead of emphasizing relationships or functions, the sequence format highlights the chronology of events or procedures, much like a program evaluation and review technique (PERT) chart (see figure 5). A common management tool, the PERT diagram offers a graphic display of the sequence of activities for a given project. Both hierarchies and sequences allow for drawing connections between concepts vertically or horizontally, a flexible aspect of this organizational scheme that the traditional outline cannot match.

FIGURE 4
HIERARCHY OF MODELS FOR IMPROVING COLLEGE TEACHING

Assessment/ Feedback	Discussion/ Sharing	Dissemination	Clinical/ Development	Teaching/ Learning	Instructional Planning
Faculty Inventory of Good Practice	Great Teachers Seminar	Centers for Improving Teaching	Instructional Skills Workshop	Cognitive Instructional Intervention	Instructional Event Design
Two-Dimensional Model	Academic Alliances	Publications		Training for Information Processing	Educational Program Development
Five-Step Process					
				Multiple Intelligences & Teaching	
Classroom Assessment					
				Experiential Learning & 4MAT	
				Integrating Teaching & Learning Styles	

Application of the model

The basic procedure for organizing information in this model, whether a hierarchy or a sequence, requires that major topics be identified first, which will assist in determining a preliminary design to use. Generally, these topics are what DuBois called "repeatable categories," a group of five to seven concepts basic to the lesson's main subject. Once these topics are determined, patterns—the key to organizing the information—should begin to emerge. Hence, one should try to recognize the appropriate patterns in advance of actually placing the pertinent information into an organizational design.

Although the whole process may seem a bit cumbersome at first, the resulting notes for a lecture or for studying are much more lucid. Moreover, the all-important connections that are often missed in learning information actually become part of the content with this model. Once the skill is acquired of selecting appropriate designs and committing the concepts to the chosen designs, the procedure can become somewhat instinctive. According to DuBois, learners skilled in this technique do not even require a knowledge of the subject to organize the content as it is presented, and

FIGURE 5

EXAMPLE OF A SIMPLE PERT DIAGRAM

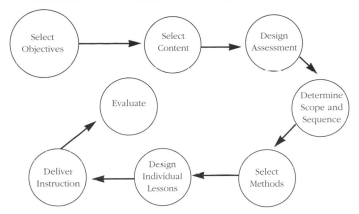

students' use of this model can actually enable them to pre-
dict test questions.

Most important, however, this model can help learners
develop a better understanding of the content for greater
application of the knowledge gained. Faculty as well as
students can apply the model, as it is relevant to organizing
information for both presentations and notes. And faculty
members' use of the model can actually help students develop these organizing skills. Thus, teaching and learning
can both improve.

The utility of information processing
Studies of mind mapping and other more visually organized
forms for learning information recently have been published
more frequently, but coverage of this particular model is still
lacking in the literature. Although DuBois's work appears to
be somewhat limited as well (1986), his model may warrant
further examination and consideration, especially given the
appearance of similar models, such as mind mapping (Buzan
1989) and electronic organizers (Anderson-Inman 1989).

Multiple Intelligences and Teaching
The advent of theoretical explanations about the various
ways that people learn has provided critical insight for
understanding the learning process. Nevertheless, this
insight can be both helpful and troublesome for educators
and students. Current educational programs generally are

not designed to address the variations in learning students bring to the classroom, and faculty and students alike must continue to operate as though everyone learned identically, knowing the opposite is more likely the case.

The proposition that specific influences, such as music, language, and kinesics, are significant regulators of learning has altered our thinking about how the business of learning should be conducted (Gardner 1983). According to Gardner, people have learning abilities, or intelligences, that can facilitate learning in one context and inhibit the process in others. He originally identified six intelligences (1983)—linguistic, logical-mathematical, spatial, musical, bodily-kinesthetic, and personal—and later split personal into interpersonal and intrapersonal (1993).

Although everyone might actually have access to all seven intelligences, the possibility exists that a person can demonstrate an exceptional skill in applying one or possibly two particular intelligences. Poets are "exemplars of linguistic intelligence"; scientists and mathematicians would be considered strong in logical-mathematical intelligence. Spatial intelligence can be manifested in sailors, surgeons, and artists, while a child prodigy like Mozart clearly represents superior musical intelligence. Athletes and dancers similarly excel presumably because of their bodily-kinesthetic intelligence. The remaining two personal intelligences can be indicative of a teacher who relates well to other people, or an actor whose self-awareness can bring about unusual capabilities for performance (Gardner 1993).

Teaching with the Seven Intelligences
The application of these seven types of intellectual prowess to classroom instruction is a natural progression. By implementing techniques to enrich all the intelligences in students while involving each intelligence in instruction, faculty can help students improve learning skills. To facilitate the employment of Gardner's theory in the classroom, Lazear (1991) devised a model for faculty to incorporate the multiple intelligences in three different ways: teaching content that applies to each of the intelligences, using the intelligences as a guide for teaching styles or methods, and involving the theory of intelligences as actual instructional content.

Although Lazear's model seems to have been designed for elementary and secondary teachers, his work may provide an additional approach for understanding Gardner's theories. Further, Lazear's practical techniques can help faculty more readily apply the intelligences theories to the college classroom. Both Gardner and Lazear advocated the development of all seven intelligences, in preference to the enhancement of a particularly strong one. Learning in college can be delayed somewhat, however, by attempting to improve learning skills in all of the intelligences. Hence, college instruction perhaps can be enhanced most with the intelligences theories by applying Lazear's second option, that of designing teaching methods with the dominant intelligences of students in mind.

For example, mathematics has been taught frequently by instructors with a strong logical-mathematical intelligence in a manner most directly suited to students who also appear dominant in the logical-mathematical category. Nevertheless, if the majority of students in class are weak in this particular intelligence, their opportunities for success in mathematics are characteristically reduced, along with their ultimate interest in the subject. Except for students who will need to develop their logical-mathematical capabilities, such as mathematics and science majors, the use of teaching methods that apply directly to students' dominant intelligences seems to make more sense, especially because it could increase students' achievement in an important subject area. Thus, faculty in such a situation may be advised to consider instruction that involves more visual images, descriptive statements for the concepts, and activities like weight lifting.

Gardner's model is "a very useful and stimulating contribution to the intelligence controversy. "This book begins to set aright the heavily parochial psychological view of intelligence as uniquely or exclusively logical and verbal.

Intelligent learning

The impact of Gardner's research is demonstrated in a number of reviews published since the intelligences theories were presented. Gardner's model is "a very useful and stimulating contribution to the intelligence controversy [that] I recommend . . . enthusiastically" (Bouchard 1984, p. 508). "This book begins to set aright the heavily parochial psychological view of intelligence as uniquely or exclusively logical and verbal. . . . [Gardner's] reasoning is astute and subtle" (Bornstein 1986, p. 121).

Yet Gardner has been accused of avoiding more defined aspects of his theories (Sutherland 1984). Nevertheless, incorporating abilities previously ignored by intelligence tests is an important contribution of Gardner's work (Carroll 1984;

Eisenmann 1984). Suggesting that Gardner wrote his book for a general audience, Carroll indicated that his work substantiates a theory of multiple intelligences that had been hypothesized for some time. And he developed his theories "with consummate humanistic scholarship and artistry but also with considerable attention to scientific underpinnings and to implications for the attainment of societal goals" (Carroll 1984, p. 865). Notwithstanding the apparent recognition of Gardner's work, the overall impact of his intelligences theory has not yet been felt universally in education.

While Gardner did not equate multiple intelligences with theories of learning styles, both approaches to understanding learning emphasize the influence of characteristics that cause people to learn in different ways and at different rates. Gardner's position was that learners can use one or more of the Seven Intelligences in each learning situation, while learning styles suggest a general attitude or perspective toward learning. For example, someone referred to as "an abstract learner" would tend to apply abstract thinking in all learning situations, according to theories of learning styles. Yet even with learning styles, individual variations and periodic alterations in style are common (McKeachie 1995). No matter which theoretical position is preferred, though, the critical issue for faculty is that both concepts focus on "the fact that learners differ and that we need to take account of these differences in teaching" (McKeachie 1995, p. 1).

Experiential Learning and 4MAT

Consequentially distinct from Gardner's intelligences theories are the various representations of learning styles. Although relatively recent, research in learning styles already has established its own niche in educational research (Claxton and Murrell 1987; Claxton and Ralston 1978). Some of the research on learning styles led to the development of the Experiential Learning model (Kolb 1984) and the 4MAT instructional model that incorporates Kolb's concepts. Both are intended to influence classroom activities to allow for the variations in students' capabilities and experiences.

The Experiential Learning Cycle

Based on extensive research in learning styles, brain hemisphere dominance, and student experience, Kolb (1984) designed a model that consists of a framework for understanding the influence of experience and personality on the process of learning. This orientation is elemental in his model, as Kolb theorized that learning cannot be reduced merely to a set of outcomes. Instead, he suggested that learning must be regarded as a perpetual activity based on situations in life. Kolb further proposed that learning naturally moves through four phases: experience, reflection, abstraction, and experimentation (1984). Consequently, students are expected to progress through each stage of the cycle in a continuous pattern.

Essentially, Kolb's Learning Cycle describes four basic types of learners: divergent, assimilating, convergent, and accommodating. Divergent learners, who recognize precise meaning but do not lack imagination, are able to consider the alternative aspects of concrete circumstances. Linking abilities with inductive reasoning and development of logical theory, assimilating learners manipulate abstract information and ideas. Convergent learners are conversely more deductive, linking theory to practice. Finally, accommodating learners are pragmatic experimenters. They can adapt to change in the environment by replacing theory with intuition.

Identifying what specific approach appears to be dominant with any given learner is possible using Kolb's Learning Styles Inventory and the accompanying Learning-Style Profile. Although this model may appear to suggest that learners can be classified neatly into one of these four types, some students do not demonstrate a clearly dominant style. Combinations of all four classifications are possible, with dominance appearing in one or more of the types.

Beyond an understanding of the possible variations in students' learning, the research on learning styles, like Kolb's theories, can provide faculty with insight for adjusting their teaching to enhance the learning of their diverse student population. This brief description of Kolb's model is included to provide the basis for some applications of the Learning Cycle in the college classroom (see Claxton and Murrell 1987 and Claxton and Ralston 1978 for a more complete account of Kolb's work).

The Learning Cycle goes to class

To apply Kolb's model directly to the design and assessment of classroom activities, Svinicki and Dixon (1987) introduced an extension to the four-phase cycle. Classroom techniques were suggested for each phase to provide students with appropriate situations to enrich their respective approach to learning. Methods involving laboratories, films, and readings are among those that address the experience phase. For reflection, activities like logs and journals, discussion sessions, and the use of questioning strategies seem appropriate. Lectures, papers, and projects are examples of techniques that apply to abstraction. And lessons incorporating simulations, case studies, and field work offer opportunities for experimentation as the cycle reverts to experience.

These recommended instructional techniques are just a few of the ones Svinicki and Dixon offered to implement Kolb's theories in the classroom. Because the four phases of the Learning Cycle are interconnected, some particular methods also can be applied to two or more phases. The specific goal of instruction and the idiosyncrasies of different disciplines are expected to guide the selection of activities accordingly (Duffy and Jones 1995; Erickson and Strommer 1991; Schoenfeld and Magnan 1994).

4MAT

Another application of Kolb's model is intended to bring the utility of the Experiential Learning Cycle to the classroom, much like Svinicki and Dixon did. The 4MAT® System incorporates Kolb's model, including the research in learning styles and right-left mode, as well as Kolb's Learning Styles Inventory. An additional instrument, the Learning-Type Measure, has also been developed more recently by McCarthy and St. Germain (1993). The intent of the 4MAT model is to enhance an instructor's awareness of the relative nature of learning. Moreover, the model provides faculty with a flexible instructional method to address the variances in students' learning styles (McCarthy 1986). Primarily directed at elementary and secondary educators, 4MAT training, as provided by Excel (see Appendix B for the address), has also addressed the diversity of students and learning applications in everyday life for college faculty and corporate trainers.

The Learning Styles Inventory and the Learning-Style Profile can be used to assess the individuality of students' learning styles (Kolb 1984). (The addition by Excel of the self-report Learning-Type Measure can enable learners to determine more of the subtle differences in individual behavior preferences.) Following completion of the inventory, students can be categorized based on their relatively dominant learning styles, recognizing, of course, that a strict adherence to categories is unwise considering the range of variability within each quadrant of the model. Because 4MAT is designed primarily for specific faculty interventions, four techniques are incorporated in the model to facilitate the instruction for each of the four basic types of learner.

Faculty interventions. Given that divergent learners require concrete information, faculty should realize that these learners expect to obtain reasons for everything. Assimilating learners, who match facts with their own observations, expect to receive factual information. Practical convergent learners need to link theory to practice and will naturally want an opportunity to test or experiment. Faculty need to allow accommodating learners, who relate experience to application, time to teach themselves as well as others (McCarthy 1986).

The role of faculty should consequently change throughout the phases of the Learning Cycle. The divergent learner depends on the instructor to be a motivator. Conversely, instructors of assimilating learners would be expected to be disseminators of information. Convergent learners need faculty to serve as facilitators or coaches. For the self-motivated accommodating learners immersed in discovery, faculty need to serve as resource specialists. Hence, faculty tend to be more directly involved in instruction for the first two types of learners, while the last two groups of students tend to take more control of their learning. Faculty who use this model should remember, however, that students should proceed through the entire cycle and not concentrate within any one quadrant. Similarly, both brain hemispheres need to be engaged, thus enhancing the weaker capabilities (Scott 1994).

4MAT for success. Perhaps to Kolb's credit, the 4MAT model has achieved extensive recognition and presumably similar use. McCarthy and the Excel corporation she established have been instrumental in disseminating the model. The 4MAT® System has been implemented by state staff developers in North Carolina, Texas, Florida, and Louisiana; both urban and suburban school districts; Mary Baldwin College in Virginia; the University of North Carolina at Chapel Hill; the University of Nebraska at Omaha; and the Ministry of Education in Singapore. Excel also has conducted training for "thousands from educational, government, and private organizations in the effective application of this innovative learning model."*

Numerous reports of successful experiences with the model have been published. Faculty who learned 4MAT have been more inclined to interact with one another as they became more aware of different learning styles, especially their own, and even have used the model for designing lessons (Blair and Judah 1990). Students have benefited from using the model as well. Generally, the development of conceptual knowledge and application has improved when students have used the model in their work (Allyn 1989; Kelly 1990; Wilkerson and White 1988). Students' attitudes toward learning have also improved markedly when the model is implemented (Kelly 1990; Weber and Weber 1990; Wilkerson and White 1988).

One reviewer found "no direct criticism of the 4MAT model in the literature" (Scott 1994, p. 10), noting as well the comprehensive applicability of the model at all institutional levels and a "widespread use [that] supports the conclusion that 4MAT deserves high marks [for] the criterion of *fruitfulness"* (p. 12). After applying the model, one faculty member commented that "student interest and motivation were high and . . . they learned the concepts quicker and retained them longer" (Blair and Judah 1990, p. 38). Obtaining knowledge of learning styles has given faculty numerous advantages (Blair and Judah 1990; Kelley 1990; Kelly 1990). "Overall, 4MAT has been an incredibly useful tool. It has helped me understand and communicate with others in every aspect of my life" (Kelly 1990, p. 40).

Integrating Teaching and Learning Styles
Based on his own research with learning styles, Grasha (1983) also devised a model that links the insight gained from examining learning styles to applications for teaching. "A considerable amount of empirical data has been gathered on the major approaches to learning style. *What such models suggest about teaching and learning processes ought to be a part of our conceptual base*" (Grasha 1996, p. 126). He also

---

*Ziona Friedlander 1995, personal communication.

advocated the use of learning style models that can inform decisions about teaching styles.

Based on research at the University of Cincinnati is a construct for detecting students' preferred style of communication with fellow students and faculty (Reichmann and Grasha 1974). Six styles have been identified, describing students as avoidant, collaborative, competitive, dependent, independent, and participant (Reichmann and Grasha). This learning style model is presented here as the basis of a model that integrates these learning styles with corresponding teaching styles (Grasha 1996).

Teaching styles

As he had done earlier with Reichmann, Grasha designed a process for describing and determining teaching styles. His definition for teaching styles specified "a pattern of needs, beliefs, and behaviors that faculty displayed in their classroom" (Grasha 1996, p. 152), and he perceived these styles to involve an interrelated set of teaching behaviors, including administration of curriculum, subject orientation, content presentation, classroom management, and student contact and guidance. In an attempt to capture the essence of faculty demeanor in the classroom, Grasha determined that five distinct styles were prevalent in college teaching: delegator, expert, facilitator, formal authority, and personal model. He further suggested that these teaching styles "interact in predictable ways with the learning styles of students" (p. 153).

Recognizing that classifying individuals with descriptors of this type was not sensible, Grasha indicated that college faculty display all of these styles to some extent. Primarily, faculty tend to teach in ways that can be described with combinations of the five teaching styles. Thus, Grasha (1996) defined four combinations, or clusters, that depict faculty behavior in the classroom: expert/formal authority, personal model/expert/formal authority, facilitator/personal model/ expert, and delegator/facilitator/expert. The arrangement of each cluster suggests the degree of influence of the particular styles. For example, a faculty member who teaches as a facilitator/personal model/expert will help students find necessary information before conducting a demonstration or presenting the information.

Similarly, particular teaching methods are related to certain style clusters. Hence, the delegator/facilitator/expert would

Grasha defined four combinations, or clusters, that depict faculty behavior in the classroom: expert/formal authority, personal model/ expert/formal authority, facilitator/pers onal model/ expert, and delegator/facili tator/expert.

tend to incorporate contracts, seminars, and independent study, while the expert/formal authority relies on lectures, exams, and controlled discussions. Similarly, the personal model/expert/formal authority might use personal experiences and demonstrations, and the facilitator/personal model/expert may prefer case studies, flexible discussions, and simulations (Grasha 1996).

The connections between the teaching style clusters and similar combinations of learning styles are also included in the model. Thus, the expert/formal authority instructor tends to be most compatible with the dependent/participant/competitive learner. Likewise, personal model/expert/formal authority instructors can be matched with participant/dependent/collaborative students, facilitator/personal model/expert faculty with collaborative/participant/independent learners, and delegator/facilitator/experts with independent/collaborative/participants (Grasha 1996).

Styles as facilitators of learning

Grasha's model for integrating teaching and learning styles was designed to provide faculty with a tool for using both types of style to improve teaching and learning. While striving for compatible style combinations is this model's goal, a deliberate attempt to work with a mismatch in styles can also offer a valuable developmental opportunity (Grasha 1996), much like Gardner advocated the enhancement of one's weaker intelligences. Generally, however, faculty are expected to use this model to help them become more sensitive to students' learning styles and to adapt their instruction accordingly. Such changes should be implemented gradually, without expecting a quick or easy effort (Grasha 1996).

The recent development of this integrated model understandably precludes much commentary on its potential, much less on any evaluations of its use. Even so, some professionals have reacted to it favorably, noting the combination of teaching styles and methods to improve learning. "In this time of increasing emphasis on learning outcomes, [this] work provides faculty with a guide for both enhancing student learning and making their teaching more fulfilling" (Grasha 1996, back cover). The model offers faculty an opportunity to learn more about their students and themselves as they use Grasha's model to make their teaching more innovative.

A Related Technique: Effective Classroom Questioning

A group of classroom techniques often associated with learning theory, questioning strategies lack the singular form that helps to define the models in this report. Widely referenced in many formats, no single approach to questioning students appears predominant. Even so, this technique remains an important skill for all faculty.

As teaching and learning have begun a transition away from lower-level cognitive skills, such as simple recall, the development of thinking skills has taken on renewed importance. Even the private sector is emphasizing the need for more attention in schools on thinking and problem solving. Among the most effective methods for fostering students' thinking is an ancient art, that of questioning. While no single instructional model providing suggestions for competent questioning appears to be distinctly invaluable, some especially helpful strategies have been offered.

Three organizational techniques are helpful in designing questions for the classroom: Bloom's taxonomy, Aschner-Gallagher's system, and Dantonio's questioning processes (Hansen 1994). Bloom's taxonomy (1956) was designed to provide a system for classifying educational objectives into six separate categories: knowledge, comprehension, application, analysis, synthesis, and evaluation. Knowledge refers to the simple process of recalling information, comprehension involves understanding the information learned, and application involves the possible uses of this information, often in new situations. A student uses analysis to determine the reasoning or individual aspects of an argument or problem and synthesis to design or develop a new approach to solving a particular problem. Judgment is the result of evaluation.

Sanders (1966), who based his questioning model on Bloom's taxonomy, suggests that instructional questions should be constructed to transcend simple probes of memory. His model for designing questions uses seven categories: memory, translation, interpretation, application, analysis, synthesis, and evaluation. Sanders replaced Bloom's category of knowledge with memory, which he said is more related to an intellectual activity, similar to the other designations. He also split Bloom's category of comprehension into two categories, translation and interpretation. Translation is the one aspect of comprehension that involves the conversion of a concept into different language, and interpretation requires a student to search for relationships among concepts. (See Appendix C for examples of questions using Bloom's taxonomy and Sanders's adaptation of it.)

Using a hierarchy similar to Bloom's taxonomy, Aschner and Gallagher (1965) developed a four-level classification system incorporating questions for memory, convergent thinking, divergent thinking, and evaluation. The two categories of memory and evaluation are comparable to Bloom's classification. Convergent questions rely on background information as a basis for making objective decisions. Conversely, divergent questions can have several correct options, depending on the individual perspective considered, that may result in new information. (See Appendix C for examples of questions using Aschner-Gallagher's system.)

Dantonio's (1990) questioning processes provided the basis for organizing questions into four groups of activities: gathering, sorting, organizing, and interpreting. Within each group are more specific behaviors that further define the purpose of the question. Gathering questions can involve the student in recalling information or making observations. Sorting questions include grouping, comparing, and contrasting separate entities. Students use organizing questions to label, classify, or sequence information and interpreting questions to generate inferences and predictions. (See Appendix C for examples of questions using Dantonio's questioning processes.)

Wasserman (1992) also developed techniques for using questions in the classroom. Also incorporating the work of Bloom, Wasserman focused on the problem of weak questioning strategies, such as the closed question that requires only a brief answer. To help identify such inadequate questions, Wasserman included assessment forms to help faculty analyze their own questioning skills (see also Bonwell and Eison 1991).

Yet another valuable resource, specifically created for faculty, is *Classroom Communication* (Neff and Weimer 1989). Numerous other guides are available for faculty members' development of questioning skills. A logical first step for those who would improve their classroom questioning is a self-assessment (see Wasserman 1992), followed by a cursory review of the available literature.

INSTRUCTIONAL PLANNING MODELS

An exceedingly consequential part of the role of college faculty involves the necessary preparation for class, or instructional planning. This planning skill is often neglected, however, even in some of the rather limited preparatory coursework. Hence, faculty resort to borrowing planning schemes and ideas from colleagues. Although relatively few models for the development of faculty planning skills appear to be available, the models included in this section can be helpful to faculty who perceive a deficiency in their planning skills that cultivates disorganized or insufficient lessons.

Instructional Event Design

The work of Gagné is perhaps best known to educators in the fields of educational psychology and instructional design. His examination of the learning process led to the identification of a series of events that could influence students' learning. Calling such events "external," Gagné contrasted them with learning, which he called "an internal process." He believed that these external events are essential to the learning process and generally are planned by faculty. Consequently, Gagné devised a lesson planning model based on nine instructional events (1965, 1970).

Typically taking the form of communication, the external instructional events are designed specifically for each learning objective. Usually intended as steps to prepare learners for instruction, the first three events include securing attention, communicating objectives, and facilitating the recall of necessary knowledge (Gagné 1965, 1970). To gain students' attention, faculty may ask an interesting question, move to the front of the room, or initiate some other change in stimulus. The purpose of the learning experience is then commonly communicated, even though students sometimes may easily discern what they will be doing. Expressing this objective helps to keep both students and instructor on the subject of the day as well as to demonstrate the instructor's trustworthiness. It will also help students to better understand what is expected of them. Because much of the learning that takes place depends on prior knowledge and having recalled the knowledge at the start of the process speeds up learning, the next step is to help students with this recall. Asking students questions at this stage will facilitate the recall, even if the questions are intended to be rhetorical.

After these preliminary stages are completed, the instructor proceeds with the next two instructional events. The fourth event, information to be learned or another type of stimulus, must be connected to the expected behavior communicated earlier in the objective. The stimulus may include examples or other techniques to facilitate learning. One technique intended to assist learning is actually the fifth step, guiding students through a specific learning activity. Sometimes referred to as "guided practice," this event requires a certain amount of constraint on the part of the instructor, even though students may not always be successful in their efforts.

Once students believe that they have mastered a skill or some amount of information, the final four events occur. Students should be given an opportunity to demonstrate their learning with some kind of performance, after which the instructor should offer feedback that will help learners to improve with the next performance. Although students may often dwell on their total performance score, the essential purpose of feedback at this stage is consistent improvement. As performance improves, an assessment of learning outcomes eventually is necessary to provide a summative judgment of both learning and teaching. Finally, the knowledge gained in this process must be adequately stored for future recall and application. Instructors can help students attain both goals by providing ample opportunities to apply their new knowledge to novel situations (Gagné 1965, 1970).

Although this process may appear simplistic, faculty who have not been exposed to each step could discover an instructional event that has been missing in their teaching. The simplicity of the model might also suggest more of an application to elementary or secondary school teaching. Realistically, Gagné's model is applicable at all levels of education, primarily because of the flexibility inherent in each event.

This sequence of instructional events may seem to be a complete cycle with a fixed design, but the sequence of events can be rearranged as needed and one or more of the events deleted, depending on the subject matter and the faculty member (Gagné, Briggs, and Wager 1992). And some students may not require one or more events. As faculty proceed in their planning, they must be prepared to determine whether students will need the assistance of each learning event.

Gagné developed and refined his model over a period of 10 or more years through his texts in educational psychology and instructional design. Several reviewers have noted the value of Gagné's conceptual model for instructional design (Leonard 1975; Yoshida 1979), with the concept of necessary prerequisite learning skills a significant contribution (Goldner 1973). Gagné provided "a clearly written review of principles with a never-lost-sight-of application to learning in the real world" (Nolan 1975, p. 145). His work provides "a complete guide to developing a competency-based education program" (Gray 1979, p. 358) and "the best practical explanation of information processing as applicable to instruction" (Nolan 1975, p. 146).

Gagné's model is strikingly similar to another planning model that was, in fact, designed for public school teachers. Hunter (1994) formulated a decision-making model for lesson design that also allows for flexible implementation by teachers. Essentially, the model consists of seven elements that are comparable to many of the events in Gagné's model: anticipatory set, the lesson's objective, instructional content, modeling of expected outcomes, assessment of students' understanding, practice guided by the instructor, and independent practice. Although Hunter's model was intended for public school teachers, the planning components, like those in Gagné's model, can be useful to college faculty as well.

Educational Program Development

With a model for designing entire curricula as well as individual courses, Diamond (1989) challenged faculty to reach beyond what already exists and to consider ideal possibilities. This simple, but flexible, model essentially includes two phases: "(1) project selection and design and (2) production, implementation, and evaluation" (p. 6). The first phase is intended for use with the entire curriculum, the second for specific classes. Both phases rely on gathering data and the use of diagrams that can visually depict the sequence and relationships of each step in the process. This aspect of the model is similar to the sequencing in DuBois's model and the sample PERT diagram in figure 5.

The first phase of the model proceeds from identification of a project to consideration of ideal resources to transaction, using elements specific to the project. Each stage in phase one involves the necessary process of collecting data to inform the sequential decisions. Realistic academic priorities and the potential for success provide the basis for identifying the desired project. After the selection of a planning team, the ideal possibilities of the project are established after considering student and social characteristics, institutional or unit priorities, and the knowledge and research applicable to the selected subject field. The transaction stage moves the project from the ideal to the realistic with the necessary data about course goals, time factors, resources (personnel, supplies, funding, facilities), anticipated students, and instructional research.

The model's second phase includes selection of course objectives, evaluation design, selection of teaching methods, determination of needed supplies, pilot testing of components (if needed), implementation, assessment, and any necessary modifications. Course objectives should be measurable behavioral objectives that collectively specify the anticipated outcomes. To be adequate for instruction, behavioral objectives should describe an observable behavior, a measurable degree of expected performance, and the circumstances within which the behavior should be accomplished. For example, an objective for English grammar might be "Upon completion of this lesson, the student should be able to correctly identify the 10 nouns in a list of 25 words within two minutes."

Evaluations are then designed on the basis of these objectives to measure the actual outcomes. Decisions about teaching methods and supplies are made for each unit once the course is subdivided into units. Any new supplies, equipment, or other materials acquired should be tested on a small group of students to determine potential flaws. The entire course is then ready for experimental trial, during which assessment data are gathered and any necessary changes made in design of the course (Diamond 1989).

Course and curriculum planning is clearly a necessary stage in the instructional process. While the use of models, like the two developed by Diamond and Gagné, can facilitate planning, both authors realized the necessity to apply the planning model flexibly. Hence, faculty members should be willing to mold the model to their own specific needs.

Educators were noticeably impressed when Diamond's model appeared in the literature, calling it "a viable . . . model [that] serves as an efficient means for designing, implementing, and evaluating courses and curricula" (Munday 1990, p. 89) and "a valuable resource" (Kemp 1989, p. 55). The comprehensive nature of Diamond's work seems to be a major element (Ashton 1990; Kemp 1989). The systematic design of his model (Ashton 1990; Munday 1990) "maximizes the input of time, effort, and money" (Ashton 1990, p. 583).

Many of Bok's (1986) recommendations for improving college and university learning could also apply to Diamond's model (Kemp 1989). With extensive potential applications, including both entire curricula and individual courses, the model is a "thorough and functional procedure for improving courses and curricula" (Munday 1990, p. 91). With his "extensive experience in the field," Diamond "does the rest of us a valuable service by sharing it" (Ashton 1990, p. 584).

Another Model

Because course and lesson planning is a complex, time-consuming endeavor and the advent of computer technology has provided multiple opportunities for reducing the complexity of and time required for many tasks, the development of a computerized system for instructional planning should come as no great surprise. What does seem surprising is the apparently small contribution of technology to this aspect of college instruction and the similarly limited amount of coverage given it. Devised by Vogler (1991) and based upon his theory of Curriculum Pedagogy Assessment, the Peaks model is a series of three expert software systems (for developing courses, lessons, and exams) that serve as the delivery components of a comprehensive instructional design system, from planning through evaluation. No doubt the recent development of the model has contributed to its inadequate coverage in the literature, and no reviews of the model appear to have been written. Moreover, instructional design as a specialty in educational technology is also a rather modern development and one that might exclude typical faculty from participating in the use of instructional design programs.

CONCLUSION

Faculty have both the capability and the responsibility to consistently strive for the improvement of instruction and learning. The models highlighted in this report provide numerous opportunities for instituting or sustaining this initiative for continuing development. While tested and validated frequently at numerous sites, each model should be expected to have varying results with different instructors, classes, and institutions. Therefore, faculty may have to commit themselves to a certain degree of experimentation when using these models or any other technique for improving instruction.

Applying the Models to Improve College Teaching

Obviously, no guarantees are offered with these models. The process of experimentation, which has been so much a part of the development of these and other models, should naturally be expected in their application as well. And during experimentation, faculty will inevitably find that a number of decisions are necessary. How many models to consider, how many to implement, how often they are used, and how their use can be evaluated are just some of the concerns that may need to be addressed. Further, faculty members' individual differences in learning may tend to affect their preferences for some models. An instructor who finds the Classroom Assessment model exciting and empowering, for example, may not be as enthusiastic about Cognitive Instructional Intervention.

Because of the normally demanding role of teaching, major adjustments to instructional practices should be avoided. In fact, the advice Angelo and Cross (1993) offer with their model could be applied to any of the teaching improvement models. Faculty are wise to build success into their improvement efforts with a modest application of one model. Incremental changes to instruction are wise.

Faculty-Driven Improvement

The literature addressing organizational change includes some specific, immutable idiosyncrasies, one of which suggests the individuality of change (Fullan and Stiegelbauer 1991; Hord et al. 1987; Steeples 1990). In other words, change directed from the top is not nearly as effective as change cultivated among the ranks of those who are expected to adopt innovations. Consequently, the primary initiators of instructional improve-

Faculty members' individual differences in learning may tend to affect their preferences for some models. An instructor who finds the Classroom Assessment model exciting and empowering, for example, may not be as enthusiastic about Cognitive Instructional Intervention.

ment should understandably be faculty (Weimer 1990). In fact, as some of the models in this text suggest, faculty-driven improvement of teaching stands a much better chance of succeeding. Because they will not accommodate pressure from without to develop, faculty need to accept their own potential for improvement.

Moreover, faculty already have a commitment to students' learning, and educators enter the profession primarily because of this commitment. Yet to compensate for the graduate education that prepared them for research rather than teaching, faculty also have an obligation to promote their own learning in the discipline of college teaching (Boyer 1990).

The purpose of this report is to provide faculty with a resource that may help them meet this obligation without placing additional demands on their limited time and resources. Each model in this report was selected for its basic simplicity, both for understanding and for implementation. Hence, faculty should be able to implement most of these models without more in-depth preparation through workshops or training sessions. Although some of the models may require additional resources, including personnel, faculty have a wide range of choices in this collection. The next investment for improving college teaching should therefore be accessible.

Institutions' Implementation of the Models
As already indicated, though the point perhaps cannot be overemphasized, change within an organization is primarily an individual, very personal situation. Thus, institutions do not change, people do (Hord et al. 1987), and because of this common but often misunderstood aspect of change, the notion of any institution's adopting one or more of these models as an organizational initiative is vigorously discouraged.

Some academic leaders, in their exuberance over one of these models, may suggest its implementation by the institution. After all, if a particular idea has merit, then it reasonably should be promoted. But faculty must be allowed to consider, adopt, adapt, and experiment with these and other instructional improvement models as personal choices (Weimer 1990). Because of the intrinsic rewards inherent in the learning process and the tendency of college faculty to be motivated by these rewards, institutional support for experimentation to enhance learning should be a priority (Cross 1989).

Nevertheless, coercion for implementation of these innovations is likely to result in failure.

The Role of Administrators

Administrators who wish to support the faculty's adoption of one or more of these models must therefore try to restrain their enthusiasm yet provide the sustenance necessary for free choice among the faculty. First and foremost, information on teaching improvement models must be made available to all faculty, especially the often-forgotten part-time instructors. Faculty who decide to implement such a model should then be offered whatever support is available to ensure the potential for success with the model. According to one very wise department chair, the primary role of the instructional leader is to "remove the stones from the path of the faculty."

Clearly, faculty who have demonstrated their concern for instructional development by experimenting with teaching improvement models deserve all the support in their endeavors that administrators can offer. And leaders, like the faculty, should not anticipate rapid or widespread improved teaching and learning as a result of the implementation of the models. Such changes will take time. Consequently, support for these changes must continue or the effort may fail. If a major portion of the faculty decide to adopt such a model, the entire process can take seven years or more.

Additional Models

The collection of teaching improvement models in this report clearly does not include all such methods for instructional development. Some models may not have been developed as completely as those included in this report. In addition, the literature may not include descriptions for some models. The search for models similar to the ones included in this monograph should be ongoing, especially among faculty development professionals and programs.

Moreover, the development of teaching improvement models clearly has not yet reached its limit. The literature on college teaching abounds with ideas or tips for making instruction more effective. Yet most of these techniques lack the development necessary to turn them into models with relatively universal application in college classrooms. Like all improvement processes, the development of models for improving college teaching needs to be continuous. Consequently, this research and development should be included as a necessary part of all faculty development efforts.

Because faculty are the primary agents of change in the classroom, the responsibility to continue designing and shaping models for improving college teaching should also be shared with faculty. The commitment to perpetual instructional development is an essential aspect of the role of faculty.

APPENDIX A: College Teaching Reading List

Boice, Robert. 1992. *The New Faculty Member: Supporting and Fostering Professional Development.* San Francisco: Jossey-Bass.

Brookfield, Stephen D. 1990. *The Skillful Teacher: On Technique, Trust, and Responsiveness in the Classroom.* San Francisco: Jossey-Bass.

————. 1995. *Becoming a Critically Reflective Teacher.* San Francisco: Jossey-Bass.

Davis, Barbara G. 1993. *Tools for Teaching.* San Francisco: Jossey-Bass.

Davis, James R. 1993. *Better Teaching, More Learning: Strategies for Success in Postsecondary Settings.* Phoenix: Oryx Press.

Duffy, Donna K., and Janet W. Jones. 1995. *Teaching within the Rhythms of the Semester.* San Francisco: Jossey-Bass.

Eble, Kenneth E. 1988. *The Craft of Teaching: A Guide to Mastering the Professor's Art.* 2d ed. San Francisco: Jossey-Bass.

Erickson, Bette L., and Diane W. Strommer. 1991. *Teaching College Freshmen.* San Francisco: Jossey-Bass.

Feldman, Kenneth A., and Michael B. Paulsen, eds. 1994. *Teaching and Learning in the College Classroom.* Needham Heights, Mass.: Ginn Press.

Flood, Barbara J., and Joy K. Moll. 1990. *The Professor Business: A Teaching Primer for Faculty.* Medford, N.J.: Learned Information.

Guskey, Thomas R. 1988. *Improving Student Learning in College Classrooms.* Springfield, Ill.: Charles C Thomas.

Halpern, Diane F., and Associates. 1994. *Changing College Classrooms: New Teaching and Learning Strategies for an Increasingly Complex World.* San Francisco: Jossey-Bass.

Johnson, Glenn R. 1990. *First Steps to Excellence in College Teaching.* 3d ed. Madison, Wisc.: Magna Publications.

McKeachie, Wilbert J. 1994. *Teaching Tips: Strategies, Research, and Theory for College and University Teachers.* 9th ed. Lexington, Mass.: D.C. Heath.

Magnan, Robert, ed. 1990. *147 Practical Tips for Teaching Professors.* Madison, Wisc.: Magna Publications.

Menges, Robert J., and Marilla D. Svinicki, eds. 1991. *College Teaching: From Theory to Practice.* New Directions for Teaching and Learning No. 45. San Francisco: Jossey-Bass.

Menges, Robert J., Maryellen Weimer, and Associates. 1996. *Teaching on Solid Ground: Using Scholarship to Improve Practice.* San Francisco: Jossey-Bass.

Meyers, Chet, and Thomas B. Jones. 1993. *Promoting Active Learning: Strategies for the College Classroom.* San Francisco: Jossey-Bass.

Neff, Rose A., and Maryellen Weimer, eds. 1990. *Teaching College: Collected Readings for the New Instructor*. Madison, Wisc.: Magna Publications.

Newble, David, and Robert Cannon. 1989. *A Handbook for Teachers in Universities and Colleges: A Guide to Improving Teaching Methods*. New York: St. Martin's Press.

O'Banion, Terry, ed. 1994. *Teaching and Learning in the Community College*. Washington, D.C.: American Association of Community Colleges.

Prichard, Keith W., and R. McLaren Sawyer, eds. 1994. *Handbook of College Teaching: Theory and Applications*. Westport, Conn.: Greenwood Press.

Richlin, Laurie, ed. 1993. *Preparing Faculty for the New Conceptions of Scholarship*. New Directions for Teaching and Learning No. 54. San Francisco: Jossey-Bass.

Schoenfeld, A. Clay, and Robert Magnan. 1994. *Mentor in a Manual: Climbing the Academic Ladder to Tenure*. Madison, Wisc.: Magna Publications.

Schuster, Jack H., Daniel W. Wheeler, and Associates. 1990. *Enhancing Faculty Careers: Strategies for Development and Renewal*. San Francisco: Jossey-Bass.

Seldin, Peter, ed. 1995. *Improving College Teaching*. Bolton, Mass.: Anker Publishing.

Svinicki, Marilla D., ed. 1990. *The Changing Face of College Teaching*. New Directions for Teaching and Learning No. 42. San Francisco: Jossey-Bass.

Theall, Michael, and Jennifer Franklin, eds. 1991. *Effective Practices for Improving Teaching*. New Directions for Teaching and Learning No. 48. San Francisco: Jossey-Bass.

Vella, Jane. 1994. *Learning to Listen, Learning to Teach: The Power of Dialogue in Educating Adults*. San Francisco: Jossey-Bass.

Weimer, Maryellen. 1990. *Improving College Teaching: Strategies for Developing Instructional Effectiveness*. San Francisco: Jossey-Bass.

———. 1993. *Improving Your Classroom Teaching*. Newbury Park, Calif.: Sage.

———, ed. 1993. *Faculty as Teachers: Taking Stock of What We Know*. University Park, Penna.: National Center on Postsecondary Teaching, Learning, and Assessment.

Wright, W. Alan, and Associates. 1995. *Teaching Improvement Practices: Successful Strategies for Higher Education*. Bolton, Mass.: Anker Publishing.

APPENDIX B: Resource List

For information about the Seven Principles for Good Practice in Undergraduate Education, contact:

Seven Principles Resource Center
Winona State University
P.O. Box 5838
Winona, MN 55987-5838
Telephone: 507-457-5020; Fax: 507-457-5586

For information about *Innovation Abstracts,* contact:

National Institute for Staff and Organizational Development
Department of Educational Administration
College of Education, SZB 348
The University of Texas at Austin
Austin, TX 78712-1293
Telephone: 512-471-7545; Fax: 708-382-4510

For information about *The Teaching Professor,* contact:

Magna Publications
2718 Dryden Drive
Madison, WI 53704-3086
Telephone: 800-433-0499 or 608-246-3591; Fax: 608-246-3597

For information about *The National Teaching and Learning Forum,* contact:

Oryx Press
4041 N. Central Avenue, Suite 700
Phoenix, AZ 85012-3397
Telephone: 800-279-6799; Fax: 800-279-4663
Internet: info@oryxpress.com
On-line edition: http://www.ntlf.com

For information about the 4MAT® System, contact:

Excel, Inc.
23385 W. Old Barrington Road
Barrington, IL 60010
Telephone: 708-382-7272 or 800-822-4MAT; Fax: 708-382-4510

APPENDIX C: Sample Questions Using Classification Systems

Bloom's Taxonomy

KNOWLEDGE

Who was President during the Trail of Tears?

COMPREHENSION

Why do we ignore the last zero in multiplication?

Sanders's Adaptation

MEMORY

TRANSLATION

What does the author mean by that statement?

INTERPRETATION

What is the connection between the Fed and our economy?

APPLICATION

What is the noun in this sentence?

ANALYSIS

Where was the author going when he took "the road less traveled"?

SYNTHESIS

How can we implement this change in the institution?

EVALUATION

Who is guilty?

Aschner-Gallagher's System

MEMORY: Who was President during the Trail of Tears?

CONVERGENT THINKING: Considering the process of synthesis, what part does oxygen play?

DIVERGENT THINKING: If you had been given the authority to drop the bomb, what would you have done?

EVALUATION: Who is guilty?

Dantonio's Questioning Processes

GATHERING:

Recalling: How many people were on the plane?

Observing: What do you see on the screen?

SORTING:

Grouping: Which responses seem to fit together?

Comparing: How are Weimer's model and Lowman's model similar?

Contrasting: What are the differences between these two lines?

ORGANIZING:

Labeling: What would you call this type of behavior?

Classifying: How would you categorize this action?

Sequencing: In what order did these events take place?

INTERPRETING:

Inferring: What caused such a reaction?

Predicting: How will the jury respond?

REFERENCES

The Educational Resources Information Center (ERIC) Clearinghouse on Higher Education abstracts and indexes the current literature on higher education for inclusion in ERIC's database and
announcement in ERIC's monthly bibliographic journal, *Resources
in Education* (RIE). Most of these publications are available
through the ERIC Document Reproduction Service (EDRS). For
publications cited in this bibliography that are available from EDRS,
ordering number and price code are included. Readers who wish
to order a publication should write to the ERIC Document Reproduction Service, 3900 Wheeler Avenue, Alexandria, Virginia 22304.
(Phone orders with VISA or MasterCard are taken at 800/227-ERIC
or 703/823-0500.) When ordering, please specify the document
(ED) number. Documents are available as noted in microfiche (MF)
and paper copy (PC). If you have the price code ready when you
call EDRS, an exact price can be quoted. The last page of the latest
issue of *Resources in Education* also has the current cost, listed
by code.

Aleamoni, Lawrence M., ed. 1987. *Techniques for Evaluating and
    Improving Instruction*. New Directions for Teaching and Learn-
    ing No. 31. San Francisco: Jossey-Bass.
Allyn, Donna P. 1989. "Application of the 4MAT Model to Career
    Guidance." *Career Development Quarterly* 37: 280–87.
Anderson, John R. 1976. *Language, Memory, and Thought*. Hills-
    dale, N.J.: Erlbaum.
———. 1982. "Acquisition of Cognitive Skill." *Psychological Review*
    89: 369–406.
———. 1983. *The Architecture of Cognition*. Cambridge, Mass.:
    Harvard Univ. Press.
Anderson, John R., and Gordon H. Bower. 1973. *Human Asso-
    ciative Memory*. Washington, D.C.: V.H. Winston.
Anderson-Inman, Lynne. 1989. "Electronic Studying: Information
    Organizers to Help Students to Study 'Better' not 'Harder.' Part
    II." *Computing Teacher* 16(9): 21–23+.
Angelo, Thomas A. 1990. "Classroom Assessment: Improving Learn-
    ing Quality Where It Matters Most." In *The Changing Face of
    College Teaching*, edited by Marilla D. Svinicki. New Directions
    for Teaching and Learning No. 42. San Francisco: Jossey-Bass.
———. 1996. "Relating Exemplary Teaching to Student Learning."
    In *Honoring Exemplary Teaching*, edited by Marilla D. Svinicki
    and Robert J. Menges. New Directions for Teaching and Learn-
    ing No. 65. San Francisco: Jossey-Bass.
Angelo, Thomas A., and K. Patricia Cross. 1989. "Classroom Re-

search for Teaching Assistants." In *Teaching Assistant Training in the 1990s,* edited by Jody D. Nyquist, Robert D. Abbott, and Donald H. Wulff. New Directions for Teaching and Learning No. 39. San Francisco: Jossey-Bass.

———. 1993. *Classroom Assessment Techniques: A Handbook for College Teachers.* 2d ed. San Francisco: Jossey-Bass.

Annis, Linda F. 1989. "A Center for Teaching and Learning." Washington, D.C.: American Association of State Colleges and Universities. ED 306 855. 11 pp. MF–01; PC–01.

Aschner, Mary J., and James J. Gallagher. 1965. *A System for Classifying Thought Processes in the Context of Classroom Verbal Interaction.* Urbana: Univ. of Illinois, Institute for Research on Exceptional Children. ED 001 262. 58 pp. MF–01; PC–03.

Ashton, Patrick J. 1990. "Review of *Designing and Improving Courses and Curricula in Higher Education." Teaching Sociology* 18: 583–84.

Astin, Alexander W. 1977. *Four Critical Years: Effects of College on Beliefs, Attitudes, and Knowledge.* San Francisco: Jossey-Bass.

Austin, Ann E., and Roger G. Baldwin. 1991. *Faculty Collaboration: Enhancing the Quality of Scholarship and Teaching.* ASHE-ERIC Higher Education Report No. 7. Washington, D.C.: George Washington Univ., Graduate School of Education and Human Development. ED 346 085. 138 pp. MF–01; PC–06.

Baldwin, Roger G., and Ann E. Austin. 1995. "Faculty Collaboration in Teaching." In *Improving College Teaching,* by Peter Seldin and Associates. Bolton, Mass.: Anker Publishing.

Barr, Robert B., and John Tagg. 1995. "From Teaching to Learning: A New Paradigm for Undergraduate Education." *Change* 27(6): 12–25.

Barsi, Louis M. 1991. "Some Illustrative Vignettes on the Uses of the Seven Principles and the Faculty and Institutional Inventories." In *Applying the Seven Principles for Good Practice in Undergraduate Education,* edited by Arthur W. Chickering and Zelda F. Gamson. New Directions for Teaching and Learning No. 47. San Francisco: Jossey-Bass.

Bass, Randall. 1993. "Higher Education's Amateur Hour: Underpreparing the Future Professoriat." *Liberal Education* 79(2): 26–31.

Berry, Elizabeth, Marilyn Filbeck, Carrie Rothstein-Fisch, and Helen Saltman. 1991. "Implementing Classroom Research in a State University: A Developmental Process." In *Classroom Research: Early Lessons from Success,* edited by Thomas Angelo. New Directions for Teaching and Learning No. 46. San Francisco: Jossey-Bass.

Bérubé, Michael. 1996. "Public Perceptions of Universities and Faculty." *Academe* 82(4): 10–17.

Black, John B. 1984. "Review of *The Architecture of Cognition.*" *Contemporary Psychology* 29: 853–54.

Blair, Dee, and Sherry S. Judah. 1990. "Need a Strong Foundation for an Interdisciplinary Program? Try 4MAT." *Educational Leadership* 48(2): 37–38.

Blake, Robert R., and Jane S. Mouton. 1985. *The Managerial Grid III.* Houston: Gulf Publishing.

Bloom, Benjamin S., ed. 1956. *Taxonomy of Educational Objectives: The Classification of Educational Goals.* New York: McKay.

Bloom, Benjamin S., J. Thomas Hastings, and George F. Madaus. 1971. *Handbook on Formative and Summative Evaluation of Student Learning.* New York: McGraw-Hill.

Bloor, Earl G. 1987. "The Instructional Skills Workshop: A Mechanism for Instructional and Organizational Renewal." *Innovation Abstracts* 9(10): 1–2. ED 291 418. 58 pp. MF–01; PC–03.

Boice, Robert. 1992. *The New Faculty Member: Supporting and Fostering Professional Development.* San Francisco: Jossey-Bass.

Bok, Derek. 1986. *Higher Learning.* Cambridge, Mass.: Harvard Univ. Press.

Bonwell, Charles C., and James A. Eison. 1991. *Active Learning: Creating Excitement in the Classroom.* ASHE-ERIC Higher Education Report No. 1. Washington, D.C.: George Washington Univ., Graduate School of Education and Human Development. ED 336 049. 121 pp. MF–01; PC–05.

Bornstein, Marc H. 1986. "Review of *Frames of Mind: The Theory of Multiple Intelligences.*" *Journal of Aesthetic Education* 20(2): 120–22.

Bouchard, Thomas J., Jr. 1984. "Review of *Frames of Mind: The Theory of Multiple Intelligences.*" *American Journal of Orthopsychiatry* 54: 506–8.

Boyer, Ernest L. 1990. *Scholarship Reconsidered: Priorities of the Professoriate.* Princeton, N.J.: Carnegie Foundation for the Advancement of Teaching. ED 326 149. 151 pp. MF–01; PC not available EDRS.

Braskamp, Larry A., and John C. Ory. 1994. *Assessing Faculty Work: Enhancing Individual and Institutional Performance.* San Francisco: Jossey-Bass.

Brinko, Kathleen T. 1991. "The Interactions of Teaching Improvement." In *Effective Practices for Improving Teaching,* edited by Michael Theall and Jennifer Franklin. New Directions for Teaching and Learning No. 48. San Francisco: Jossey-Bass.

Brookfield, Stephen D. 1995. *Becoming a Critically Reflective Teacher.* San Francisco: Jossey-Bass.

Bruner, Jerome S. 1966. *Toward a Theory of Instruction.* Cambridge, Mass.: Harvard Univ. Press.

Buzan, Tony. 1989. *Use Both Sides of Your Brain.* New York: Penguin.

Cannon, John. 1989. "Teaching History at University." *History Teacher* 22: 245–75.

Carroll, J. Gregory, and Evan G. Pattishall. 1986. "Peer Teaching Consultants: A Collegial Approach to Improve University Teaching." Paper presented at Improving University Teaching, 12th International Conference, July 15–18, Heidelberg, Germany. ED 278 308. 131 pp. MF–01; PC–06.

Carroll, John B. 1984. "An Artful Perspective on Talents." *Contemporary Psychology* 29: 864–66.

Centra, John A. 1993. *Reflective Faculty Evaluation: Enhancing Teaching and Determining Faculty Effectiveness.* San Francisco: Jossey-Bass.

Chickering, Arthur W., and Zelda F. Gamson. 1987. "Seven Principles for Good Practice in Undergraduate Education." *AAHE Bulletin* 39(7): 3–7.

———. 1991. "A Brief History of the Seven Principles for Good Practice in Undergraduate Education." In *Applying the Seven Principles for Good Practice in Undergraduate Education,* edited by Arthur W. Chickering and Zelda F. Gamson. New Directions for Teaching and Learning No. 47. San Francisco: Jossey-Bass.

Chickering, Arthur W., Zelda F. Gamson, and Louis M. Barsi. 1989. *Faculty Inventory: Seven Principles for Good Practice in Undergraduate Education.* Racine, Wisc.: Johnson Foundation.

Chism, Nancy. 1991. "Review of *Improving College Teaching.*" *Journal of Higher Education* 62: 237–39.

———. 1993. "How Faculty Develop Teaching Expertise." In *Faculty As Teachers: Taking Stock of What We Know,* edited by Maryellen Weimer. University Park: Penna.: National Center on Postsecondary Teaching, Learning, and Assessment.

Chism, Nancy V., Jane M. Fraser, and Robert L. Arnold. 1996. "Teaching Academies: Honoring and Promoting Teaching through a Community of Expertise." In *Honoring Exemplary Teaching,* edited by Marilla D. Svinicki and Robert J. Menges. New Directions for Teaching and Learning No. 65. San Francisco: Jossey-Bass.

Claxton, Charles S., and Patricia H. Murrell. 1987. *Learning Styles: Implications for Improving Educational Practices.* ASHE-ERIC

Higher Education Report No. 4. Washington, D.C.: Association
for the Study of Higher Education. ED 293 478. 116 pp. MF–01;
PC–05.

Claxton, Charles S., and Yvonne Ralston. 1978. *Learning Styles:
Their Impact on Teaching and Administration.* AAHE-ERIC
Higher Education Research Report No. 10. Washington, D.C.:
American Association for Higher Education. ED 167 065. 74 pp.
MF–01; PC–03.

Cole, Charles C., Jr. 1978. *To Improve Instruction.* AAHE-ERIC
Higher Education Research Report No. 2. Washington, D.C.:
American Association for Higher Education. ED 153 583. 89 pp.
MF–01; PC–04.

Craig, Robert T. 1978. "Cognitive Science: A New Approach to
Cognition, Language, and Communication." *Quarterly Journal
of Speech* 64: 439–50.

Crocker, Olga L., Johnny S.L. Chiu, and Cyril Charney. 1984. *Quality Circles: A Guide to Participation and Productivity.* New York:
Facts on File.

Cross, K. Patricia. 1989. "Improving Learning in Community Col-
leges." Paper prepared for a conference of the Association of
Canadian Community Colleges, May 29, Regina, Saskatchewan,
Canada. ED 308 888. 24 pp. MF–01; PC–01.

———. 1990. "Classroom Research: Helping Professors Learn More
about Teaching and Learning." In *How Administrators Can
Improve Teaching: Moving from Talk to Action in Higher
Education,* edited by Peter Seldin. San Francisco: Jossey-Bass.

———. 1996. "New Lenses on Learning." *About Campus* 1(1): 4–9.

Dantonio, Marylou. 1990. *How Can We Create Thinkers? Questioning Strategies That Work for Teachers.* Bloomington, Ind.: National Educational Service.

Davis, Barbara G. 1993. *Tools for Teaching.* San Francisco: Jossey-
Bass.

Diamond, Robert M. 1989. *Designing and Improving Courses and
Curricula in Higher Education: A Systematic Approach.* San
Francisco: Jossey-Bass.

Dinham, Sarah M. 1996. "What College Teachers Need to Know."
In *Teaching on Solid Ground: Using Scholarship to Improve
Practice,* by Robert J. Menges, Maryellen Weimer, and Asso-
ciates. San Francisco: Jossey-Bass.

DuBois, Nelson F. *n.d.* "Learning Strategy Training: An Information
Processing Perspective." Oneonta, N.Y.: State Univ. of New
York. Unpublished manuscript.

———. 1986. "A Review of the Research on Notetaking from

Lecture: Some New Directions to Investigate." Washington, D.C.: Paper presented at the 94th Annual Convention of the American Psychological Association. ED 274 896. 19 pp. MF–01; PC–01.

DuBois, Nelson F., George F. Alverson, and Richard K. Staley. 1979. *Educational Psychology and Instructional Decisions.* Homewood, Ill.: Dorsey Press.

Duffy, Donna K., and Janet W. Jones. 1995. *Teaching within the Rhythms of the Semester.* San Francisco: Jossey-Bass.

Eble, Kenneth E. 1983. *The Aims of College Teaching.* San Francisco: Jossey-Bass.

———. 1988. *The Craft of Teaching: A Guide to Mastering the Professor's Art.* 2d ed. San Francisco: Jossey-Bass.

Edgerton, Russell, Patricia Hutchings, and Kathleen Quinlan. 1991. *The Teaching Portfolio: Capturing the Scholarship in Teaching.* Washington, D.C.: American Association for Higher Education. ED 353 892. 62 pp. MF–01; PC not available EDRS.

Eisenmann, Linda. 1984. "Neuropsychology Sheds New Light on Intelligence." *American School Board Journal* 171(7): 5+.

Erickson, Bette L., and Diane W. Strommer. 1991. *Teaching College Freshmen.* San Francisco: Jossey-Bass.

Feldman, Kenneth A., and Theodore M. Newcomb. 1969. *The Impact of College on Students.* San Francisco: Jossey-Bass.

Feldman, Kenneth A., and Michael B. Paulsen, eds. 1994. *Teaching and Learning in the College Classroom.* Needham Heights, Mass.: Ginn Press.

Ferren, Ann, and William Geller. 1983. "Classroom Consultants: Colleagues Helping Colleagues." *Improving College and University Teaching* 31(2): 82–86.

Fink, L. Dee. 1989. "The Lecture: Analyzing and Improving Its Effectiveness." In *The Department Chairperson's Role in Enhancing College Teaching,* edited by Ann F. Lucas. New Directions for Teaching and Learning No. 37. San Francisco: Jossey-Bass.

Flanders, Ned A. 1970. *Analyzing Teaching Behavior.* Reading, Mass.: Addison-Wesley.

Flood, Barbara J., and Joy K. Moll. 1990. *The Professor Business: A Teaching Primer for Faculty.* Medford, N.J.: Learned Information.

Frederick, Peter J. 1989. "Involving Students More Actively in the Classroom." In *The Department Chairperson's Role in Enhancing College Teaching,* edited by Ann F. Lucas. New Directions for Teaching and Learning No. 37. San Francisco: Jossey-Bass.

Fullan, Michael G., and Suzanne Stiegelbauer. 1991. *The New Meaning of Educational Change.* 2d ed. New York: Teachers College Press.

Gaff, Jerry G. 1975. *Toward Faculty Renewal: Advances in Faculty, Instructional, and Organizational Development*. San Francisco: Jossey-Bass.

―――. 1978. "Overcoming Faculty Resistance." In *Institutional Renewal through the Improvement of Teaching,* edited by Jerry G. Gaff. New Directions for Higher Education No. 4. San Francisco: Jossey-Bass.

Gagné, Robert M. 1965. *The Conditions of Learning*. New York: Holt, Rinehart & Winston.

―――. 1970. *The Conditions of Learning*. 2d ed. New York: Holt, Rinehart & Winston.

Gagné, Robert M., Leslie J. Briggs, and Walter W. Wager. 1992. *Principles of Instructional Design*. 4th ed. Fort Worth: Harcourt Brace Jovanovich.

Gardiner, Lion F. 1994. *Redesigning Higher Education: Producing Dramatic Gains in Student Learning*. ASHE-ERIC Higher Education Report No. 7. Washington, D.C.: George Washington Univ., Graduate School of Education and Human Development. ED394442.

Gardner, Howard. 1983. *Frames of Mind: The Theory of Multiple Intelligences*. New York: Basic Books.

―――. 1993. *Multiple Intelligences: The Theory in Practice*. New York: Basic Books.

Garrison, Roger H. 1969. "1969 Seminar for Great Teachers." *Junior College Journal* 40(3): 7–9.

Gaudiani, Claire. 1985. "Local Communities of Inquiry: Penn's Academic Alliances Program." In *College-School Collaboration: Appraising the Major Approaches,* edited by William T. Daly. New Directions for Teaching and Learning No. 24. San Francisco: Jossey-Bass.

―――. 1990. "Critical Connection: School/College Faculty Alliances." *Thought and Action* 6(1): 47–50.

Gaudiani, Claire, and David G. Burnett. 1986. *Academic Alliances: A New Approach to School/College Collaboration*. Current Issues in Higher Education No. 1. Washington, D.C.: American Association for Higher Education. ED 276 383. 36 pp. MF–01; PC–02.

Gaudiani, Claire, Clara Krug, and Debra Slaughter. 1984. "Academic Alliances: School/College Faculty Collaboratives." *Foreign Language Annals* 17: 605–9.

Glasser, William. 1990. *The Quality School: Managing Students without Coercion*. New York: Harper Collins.

Glazer, Judith S. 1993. "The Doctor of Arts: Retrospect and Prospect." In *Preparing Faculty for the New Conceptions of*

Scholarship, edited by Laurie Richlin. New Directions for
Teaching and Learning No. 54. San Francisco: Jossey-Bass.

Goldner, Ralph H. 1973. "Research Report: Learning Has Pre-
requisites." *Instructor* 82(6): 24.

Gottshall, David B. 1993. *The History and Nature of the National
Great Teachers Movement.* Glen Ellyn, Ill.: College of DuPage.

Grasha, Anthony F. 1983. "Learning Styles: The Journey from
Greenwich Observatory (1796) to the College Classroom
(1983)." *Improving College and University Teaching* 32: 46–53.

———. 1996. *Teaching with Style: A Practical Guide to Enhancing
Learning by Understanding Teaching and Learning Styles.*
Pittsburgh: Alliance Publishers.

Gray, George T. 1979. "Professional References: Conditions for
Successful Learning." *Curriculum Review* 18: 358–59.

Group for Human Development in Higher Education. 1974. *Faculty
Development in a Time of Retrenchment.* New Rochelle, N.Y.:
Change Publications.

Gullette, Margaret M., ed. 1984. *The Art and Craft of Teaching.*
Cambridge, Mass.: Harvard Univ. Press.

Guskey, Thomas R. 1988. *Improving Student Learning in College
Classrooms.* Springfield, Ill.: Charles C Thomas.

Guskey, Thomas R., Don Barshis, and John Q. Easton. 1982. *The
Center for the Improvement of Teaching and Learning: Exploring
New Directions in Community College Research.* Chicago: Chi-
cago City Colleges, Center for the Improvement of Teaching and
Learning. ED 214 573. 20 pp. MF–01; PC–01.

Halpern, Diane F. 1994. "Rethinking College Instruction for a
Changing World." In *Changing College Classrooms: New Teaching and Learning Strategies for an Increasingly Complex World,*
by Diane F. Halpern and Associates. San Francisco: Jossey-Bass.

Halpern, Diane F., and Associates. 1994. *Changing College Classrooms: New Teaching and Learning Strategies for an Increasingly Complex World.* San Francisco: Jossey-Bass.

Hansen, C. Bobbi. 1994. "Questioning Techniques for the Active
Classroom." In *Changing College Classrooms: New Teaching and
Learning Strategies for an Increasingly Complex World,* by Diane
F. Halpern and Associates. San Francisco: Jossey-Bass.

Hatfield, Susan R. 1995. *The Seven Principles in Action: Improving
Undergraduate Education.* Bolton, Mass.: Anker Publishing.

Heppner, P. Paul, and Joseph A. Johnston. 1994. "Peer Consultation: Faculty and Students Working Together to Improve Teaching." *Journal of Counseling and Development* 72: 492–99.

Hersey, Paul, and Kenneth H. Blanchard. 1982. *Management of*

Organizational Behavior: Utilizing Human Resources. Englewood Cliffs, N.J.: Prentice-Hall.

Hinchey, Pat. 1995. "First Things First: Clarifying Intention." *Clear-
ing House* 68: 253–56.

Hirshfield, Claire. 1984. "The Classroom Quality Circle: A Widening
Role for Students." *Innovation Abstracts* 6(12): 1–2. ED 256 383.
46 pp. MF–01; PC–02.

Hord, Shirley M., William L. Rutherford, Leslie Huling-Austin, and
Gene Hall. 1987. *Taking Charge of Change.* Alexandria, Va.:
Association for Supervision and Curriculum Development. ED
282 876. 102 pp. MF–01; PC not available EDRS.

Humphreys, W. Lee. 1990. "A Valuable Resource." *College Teaching*
38: 156–57.

Hunter, Madeline. 1994. *Enhancing Teaching.* New York: Macmillan.

Jenrette, Mardee, and Vince Napoli. 1994. *The Teaching/Learning
Enterprise: Miami-Dade Community College's Blueprint for
Change.* Bolton, Mass.: Anker Publishing.

Johnson, David W., Roger T. Johnson, and Karl A. Smith. 1991.
*Cooperative Learning: Increasing College Faculty Instructional
Productivity.* ASHE-ERIC Higher Education Report No. 4. Washington, D.C.: George Washington Univ., School of Education
and Human Development. ED 343 465. 168 pp. MF–01; PC–07.

Johnson, Glenn R. 1976. *Analyzing College Teaching.* Manchaca,
Tex.: Sterling Swift Publishing.

———. 1978. "Johnson's Cognitive Interaction Analysis System and
Computer Program." Unpublished manuscript. College Station,
Tex.: Texas A&M Univ., Center for Teaching Excellence.

Johnson, Reid, Robert D. McCormick, Joseph S. Prus, and Julia S.
Rogers. 1993. "Assessment Options for the College Major." In
*Making a Difference: Outcomes of a Decade of Assessment in
Higher Education,* by Trudy W. Banta and Associates. San
Francisco: Jossey-Bass.

Kahn, Susan, and John Simmons. 1990. "Quality Circles in Higher
Education: A Survey of Mismanagement." *CUPA Journal* 41(3):
29–34.

Keig, Larry, and Michael D. Waggoner. 1994. *Collaborative Peer
Review: The Role of Faculty in Improving College Teaching.*
ASHE-ERIC Higher Education Report No. 2. Washington, D.C.:
George Washington Univ., Graduate School of Education and
Human Development. ED 378 925. 193 pp. MF–01; PC–08.

Kelley, Lynn S. 1990. "Using 4MAT to Improve Staff Development,
Curriculum Assessment, and Planning." *Educational Leadership*
48(2): 38–39.

Kelly, Cynthia. 1990. "Using 4MAT in Law School." *Educational Leadership* 48(2): 40–41.

Kemp, Jerrold E. 1989. "Review of *Designing and Improving Courses and Curricula in Higher Education.*" *Educational Technology* 29(5): 55–56.

Kerschner, Lee R., and Jacquelyn A.K. Kegley. 1994. "Foreword." In *Changing College Classrooms: New Teaching and Learning Strategies for an Increasingly Complex World,* by Diane F. Halpern and Associates. San Francisco: Jossey-Bass.

Kingston, Paul W. 1991. "Review of *Improving College Teaching: Strategies for Developing Instructional Effectiveness.*" *Teaching Sociology* 19: 287–88.

Kogut, Leonard S. 1984. "Quality Circles: A Japanese Management Technique for the Classroom." *Improving College and University Teaching* 32: 123–27.

Kolb, David A. 1984. *Experiential Learning: Experience as the Source of Learning and Development.* Englewood Cliffs, N.J.: Prentice-Hall.

Kort, Melissa S. 1989. "No More Band-Aids: Adult Learning and Faculty Development." A presentation to the Summer Seminar of the Association of Departments of English, July, University of Colorado–Boulder.

———. 1992. "Down from the Podium: Preparing Faculty for the Learner-Centered Classroom." In *Maintaining Faculty Excellence,* edited by Keith Kroll. New Directions for Community Colleges No. 79. San Francisco: Jossey-Bass.

Krueger, Darrell W. 1993. "Total Quality Management." In *Making a Difference: Outcomes of a Decade of Assessment in Higher Education,* by Trudy W. Banta and Associates. San Francisco: Jossey-Bass.

Krupnick, Catherine G. 1987. "The Uses of Videotape Replay." In *Teaching and the Case Method,* edited by C. Roland Christensen. Boston: Harvard Business School.

Lauridsen, Kurt. 1994. "A Contemporary View of Teaching and Learning Centers for Faculty." In *Teaching and Learning in the Community College,* by Terry O'Banion and Associates. Washington, D.C.: American Association of Community Colleges.

Laws, Priscilla. 1991. "Workshop Physics: Learning Introductory Physics by Doing It." *Change* 23(4): 20–27.

Lazear, David. 1991. *Seven Ways of Teaching: The Artistry of Teaching with Multiple Intelligences.* Palatine, Ill.: Skylight Publishing.

Lee, Calvin B.T., ed. 1967. *Improving College Teaching.* Washington, D.C.: American Council on Education.

Lehnert, Wendy G. 1984. "Review of *The Architecture of Cognition.*" *Contemporary Psychology* 29: 854–56.

Leonard, W. Patrick. 1975. "Instructional Design: An Essay Review of Three Books." *American Educational Research Journal* 12: 507–11.

Levinson-Rose, Judith, and Robert J. Menges. 1981. "Improving College Teaching: A Critical Review of Research." *Review of Educational Research* 51: 403–34.

Lewis, Karron G. 1991. "Gathering Data for the Improvement of Teaching: What Do I Need and How Do I Get It?" In *Effective Practices for Improving Teaching,* edited by Michael Theall and Jennifer Franklin. New Directions for Teaching and Learning No. 48. San Francisco: Jossey-Bass.

———, ed. 1988. *Face to Face: A Sourcebook of Individual Consultation Techniques for Faculty/Instructional Developers.* Stillwater, Okla.: New Forums Press.

Lowman, Joseph. 1984. *Mastering the Techniques of Teaching.* San Francisco: Jossey-Bass.

———. 1995. *Mastering the Techniques of Teaching.* 2d ed. San Francisco: Jossey-Bass.

Lucas, Ann F. 1994. *Strengthening Departmental Leadership: A Team-Building Guide for Chairs in Colleges and Universities.* San Francisco: Jossey-Bass.

———, ed. 1989. *The Department Chairperson's Role in Enhancing College Teaching.* New Directions for Teaching and Learning No. 37. San Francisco: Jossey-Bass.

McCarthy, Bernice. 1986. *The 4MAT System: Teaching to Learning Styles with Right/Left Mode Techniques.* Barrington, Ill.: Excel.

McCarthy, Bernice, and Clif St. Germain. 1993. *The Learning Type Measure Presenter's Manual.* Barrington, Ill.: Excel.

McCaslin, William J. 1985. "Review of *Mastering the Techniques of Teaching.*" *Teaching Sociology* 12: 494–95.

McKeachie, Wilbert J. 1994. *Teaching Tips: Strategies, Research, and Theory for College and University Teachers.* 9th ed. Lexington, Mass.: D.C. Heath.

———. 1995. "Learning Styles Can Become Learning Strategies." *National Teaching and Learning Forum* 4(6): 1–3.

McMullen, Harold G. 1982. *College Teaching Center: Inventory of Resources and Services.* 4th ed. Middletown, Va.: Lord Fairfax Community College. ED 225 635. 39 pp. MF–01; PC–02.

McNinch, George H. 1985. "Essay Review." *Journal of Research and Development in Education* 19(1): 56–57.

Maeroff, Gene I. 1983. *School and College: Partnerships in Educa-*

tion. Princeton, N.J.: Carnegie Foundation for the Advancement of Teaching. ED 238 325. 82 pp. MF–01; PC not available EDRS.

Mathis, Claude. 1984. "Review of *Mastering the Techniques of Teaching*." *Change* 16(6): 51–52.

Menges, Robert J. 1994. "Preparing New Faculty for the Future." *Thought and Action* 10(2): 81–95.

Menges, Robert J., and William C. Rando. 1996. "Feedback for Enhanced Teaching and Learning." In *Teaching on Solid Ground: Using Scholarship to Improve Practice*, by Robert J. Menges, Maryellen Weimer, and Associates. San Francisco: Jossey-Bass.

Menges, Robert J., Maryellen Weimer, and Associates. 1996. *Teaching on Solid Ground: Using Scholarship to Improve Practice*. San Francisco: Jossey-Bass.

Meyers, Chet, and Thomas B. Jones. 1993. *Promoting Active Learning: Strategies for the College Classroom*. San Francisco: Jossey-Bass.

Moore, Roy L. 1990. "Review of *Improving College Teaching*." *Journalism Educator* 45(3): 76.

Morrison, Diane. 1985. "The Instructional Skills Workshop Program: An Interinstitutional Approach." In *To Improve the Academy: Resources for Student, Faculty, and Institutional Development*, edited by Julie R. Jeffrey and Glenn R. Erickson. Stillwater, Okla.: New Forums Press. ED 344 537. 211 pp. MF–01; PC–09.

Munday, Robert. 1990. "Review of *Designing and Improving Courses and Curricula in Higher Education*." *Educational Technology Research and Development* 38(1): 89–91.

Murray, Harry G. 1987. "Acquiring Student Feedback that Improves Instruction." In *Teaching Large Classes Well*, edited by Maryellen G. Weimer. New Directions for Teaching and Learning No. 32. San Francisco: Jossey-Bass.

Murray, John P. 1995. "The Teaching Portfolio: A Tool for Department Chairpersons to Create a Climate of Teaching Excellence." *Innovative Higher Education* 19(3): 163–75.

———. Forthcoming. *Successful Faculty Development and Evaluation: The Complete Teaching Portfolio*. ASHE-ERIC Higher Education Report. Washington, D.C.: George Washington Univ., Graduate School of Education and Human Development.

National Center for Education Statistics. 1994. *A Preliminary Study of the Feasibility and Utility for National Policy of Instructional "Good Practice" Indicators in Undergraduate Education*. Washington, D.C.: U.S. Dept. of Education.

Neff, Rose A., and Maryellen Weimer. 1989. *Classroom Communication: Collected Readings for Effective Discussion and Ques-*

tioning. Madison, Wisc.: Magna Publications.

Nolan, John D. 1975. "Review of *Essentials of Learning for Instruction.*" *Teachers College Record* 77: 145–46.

Nummedal, Susan G. 1994. "How Classroom Assessment Can Improve Teaching and Learning." In *Changing College Classrooms: New Teaching and Learning Strategies for an Increasingly Complex World,* by Diane F. Halpern and Associates. San Francisco: Jossey-Bass.

Nyquist, Jody D. 1986. *CIDR: A Small Service Firm within a Research University.* Seattle: Washington Univ., Center for Instructional Development and Research. ED 297 615. 26 pp. MF–01; PC–02.

O'Banion, Terry. 1995–96. "A Learning College for the 21st Century." *Community College Journal* 66(3): 18–23.

Obler, Susan S., Julie Slark, and Linda Umbdenstock. 1993. "Classroom Assessment." In *Making a Difference: Outcomes of a Decade of Assessment in Higher Education,* by Trudy W. Banta and Associates. San Francisco: Jossey-Bass.

Pace, C. Robert. 1979. *Measuring Outcomes of College: Fifty Years of Findings and Recommendations for the Future.* San Francisco: Jossey-Bass.

Poulsen, Susan J. 1991. "Making the Best Use of the Seven Principles and Faculty and Institutional Inventories." In *Applying the Seven Principles for Good Practice in Undergraduate Education,* edited by Arthur W. Chickering and Zelda F. Gamson. New Directions for Teaching and Learning No. 47. San Francisco: Jossey-Bass.

Puyear, Don. 1990. "Review of *Improving College Teaching: Strategies for Developing Instructional Effectiveness.*" *Community, Technical, and Junior College Journal* 61(2): 58.

Quinn, Jennifer W. 1994. "If It Catches My Eye: A Report of Faculty Pedagogical Reading Habits." *Innovative Higher Education* 19(1): 53–66.

Reichmann, Sheryl W., and Anthony F. Grasha. 1974. "A Rational Approach to Developing and Assessing the Construct Validity of a Student Learning Style Scales Instrument." *Journal of Psychology* 87: 213–23.

Reinhard, Bill, and Donna Layng. 4 October 1994. "Spreading the News: For Twenty-Five Years, the National Great Teachers Movement Has Been Improving Instruction by Word of Mouth." *Community College Times* 6(19): 1+.

Romine, Larry. 1981. "Quality Circles that Enhance Productivity." *Community and Junior College Journal* 52(3): 30–31.

Sanders, Norris M. 1966. *Classroom Questions: What Kinds?* New York: Harper & Row.

Schoenfeld, A. Clay, and Robert Magnan. 1994. *Mentor in a Manual: Climbing the Academic Ladder to Tenure.* Madison, Wisc.: Magna Publications. ED 344 536. 326 pp. MF–01; PC not available EDRS.

Schuster, Jack H. 1990. "Strengthening Career Preparation for Prospective Professors." In *Enhancing Faculty Careers: Strategies for Development and Renewal,* by Jack H. Schuster, Daniel W. Wheeler, and Associates. San Francisco: Jossey-Bass.

———. 1993. "Preparing the Next Generation of Faculty: The Graduate School's Opportunity." In *Preparing Faculty for the New Conceptions of Scholarship,* edited by Laurie Richlin. New Directions for Teaching and Learning No. 54. San Francisco: Jossey-Bass.

Scott, Harry V. 1994. *A Serious Look at the 4MAT Model.* Institute, W.Va.: West Virginia State College. ED 383 654. 16 pp. MF–01; PC–01.

Seldin, Peter. 1991. *The Teaching Portfolio: A Practical Guide to Improved Performance and Promotion/Tenure Decisions.* Bolton, Mass.: Anker Publishing.

Shackelford, Ray, and Richard Henak. 1987. *Teaching the Technology of Teaching Faculty Survey.* Muncie, Ind.: Ball State University.

Shavelson, Richard J., Noreen M. Webb, and Leigh Burstein. 1986. "Measurement of Teaching." In *Handbook of Research on Teaching,* edited by Merlin C. Wittrock. 3d ed. New York: Macmillan.

Shea, Mary A. 1990. "Constructing a Compendium of Good Ideas on Teaching." *Journal of Staff, Program, and Organizational Development* 8(1): 5–16.

Shulman, Lee S. 1986. "Those Who Understand: Knowledge Growth in Teaching." *Educational Researcher* 15(2): 4–14.

———. 1987. "Knowledge and Teaching: Foundations of the New Reform." *Harvard Educational Review* 57(1): 1–22.

Siegal, Sondra. 1985. "Academic Alliances: School/College Faculty Collaboratives." *Foreign Language Annals* 18: 353–55.

Silber, Ellen, and Terre Moore. 1989. "Academic Alliances: School/College Faculty Collaboratives." *Foreign Language Annals* 22: 295–98.

Slevin, James F. 1993. "Finding Voices in the Culture of Silence." *Liberal Education* 79(2): 4–9.

Sorcinelli, Mary D. 1994. "Dealing with Troublesome Behaviors in the Classroom." In *Handbook of College Teaching: Theory and*

Applications, edited by Keith W. Prichard and R. McLaran Sawyer. Westport, Conn.: Greenwood Press.

———. 1995. "How Mentoring Programs Can Improve Teaching." In *Improving College Teaching,* by Peter Seldin and Associates. Bolton, Mass.: Anker Publishing.

Steeples, Douglas W., ed. 1990. *Managing Change in Higher Education.* New Directions for Higher Education No. 71. San Francisco: Jossey-Bass.

Stetson, Nancy E. 1991. "Implementing and Maintaining a Classroom Research Program for Faculty." In *Classroom Research: Early Lessons from Success,* edited by Thomas Angelo. New Directions for Teaching and Learning No. 46. San Francisco: Jossey-Bass.

Sutherland, Stuart. 1984. "Grand Organization in Mind." *Nature* 308: 792–93.

Svinicki, Marilla D., ed. 1990. *The Changing Face of College Teaching.* New Directions for Teaching and Learning No. 42. San Francisco: Jossey-Bass.

Svinicki, Marilla D., and Nancy M. Dixon. 1987. "The Kolb Model Modified for Classroom Activities." *College Teaching* 35(4): 141–46.

Travis, Jon. 1992. "Ocotillo: A Management Model for Technology Infusion/Implementation." *Vision* 4(2): 12–15.

Travis, Jon, Tod Outlaw, and Flo Reven. 1996. "The Preparation of the Professoriate: Graduate Programs in College Teaching." Unpublished manuscript.

Turner, Jim L., and Robert Boice. 1986. "Coping with Resistance to Faculty Development." In *To Improve the Academy: Resources for Student, Faculty, and Institutional Development,* edited by Marilla D. Svinicki, Joanne Kurfiss, and Jackie Stone. Stillwater, Okla.: New Forums Press. ED 344 538. 211 pp. MF–01; PC–09.

Vogler, Daniel E. 1991. *Performance Instruction: Planning, Delivering, Evaluating.* Eden Prairie, Minn.: Instructional Performance Systems.

Wadsworth, Emily C. 1988. *A Handbook for New Practitioners.* Stillwater, Okla.: Professional and Organizational Development Network in Higher Education.

Wallen, Carl J. 1990. "Cognition and Effective Instruction." Tempe: Arizona State Univ. Unpublished manuscript.

Wasserman, Selma. 1992. "Asking the Right Question: The Essence of Teaching." Fastback No. 343. Bloomington, Ind.: Phi Delta Kappa Educational Foundation.

Watkins, Beverly T. 11 January 1989. "Movement to Create Academic Alliances of Teachers of Same Subjects at All Education

Levels Is Growing." *Chronicle of Higher Education* 35(18):
A23–A24.

Watkins, Karen, ed. 1981. *Innovation Abstracts* 3. Austin: Univ. of
Texas, National Institute for Staff and Organizational Development. ED 212 345. 70 pp. MF–01; PC–03.

Weber, Patricia, and Fred Weber. 1990. "Using 4MAT to Improve
Student Presentations." *Educational Leadership* 48(2): 41–46.

Weimer, Maryellen. 1987. "How Do You Teach? A Checklist for
Developing Instructional Awareness." *Teaching Professor* 1(2): 3.

————. 1988. "Reading Your Way to Better Teaching." *College
Teaching* 36(2): 48–53.

————. 1990. *Improving College Teaching: Strategies for Developing
Instructional Effectiveness.* San Francisco: Jossey-Bass.

————. 1996. "Why Scholarship Is the Bedrock of Good Teaching."
In *Teaching on Solid Ground: Using Scholarship to Improve Prac-
tice,* by Robert J. Menges, Maryellen Weimer, and Associates. San
Francisco: Jossey-Bass.

Weimer, Maryellen, Joan Parrett, and Mary-Margaret Kerns. 1988.
*How Am I Teaching? Forms and Activities for Acquiring Instruc-
tional Input.* Madison, Wisc.: Magna Publications.

Weinstein, Claire E., and Richard E. Mayer. 1986. "The Teaching of
Learning Strategies." In *The Handbook of Research on Teaching,*
edited by Merlin Wittrock. New York: Macmillan.

Weinstein, Claire E., and Debra K. Meyer. 1991. "Cognitive Learning
Strategies and College Teaching." In *College Teaching: From
Theory to Practice,* edited by Robert J. Menges and Marilla D.
Svinicki. New Directions for Teaching and Learning No. 45. San
Francisco: Jossey-Bass.

Whitman, Neal A. 1988. *Peer Teaching: To Teach Is to Learn Twice.*
ASHE-ERIC Higher Education Report No. 4. Washington, D.C.:
Association for the Study of Higher Education. ED 305 016. 103
pp. MF–01; PC–05.

Wilkerson, Rhonda M., and Kinnard P. White. 1988. "Effects of the
4MAT System of Instruction on Students' Achievement, Retention, and Attitudes." *Elementary School Journal* 88: 357–68.

Wilson, Reginald. 1996. "Educating for Diversity." *About Campus*
1(2): 4–9+.

Wilson, Robert C. 1986. "Improving Faculty Teaching: Effective Use
of Student Evaluations and Consultants." *Journal of Higher
Education* 57: 196–211.

Yoshida, Roland K. 1979. "Review of *The Conditions of Learning.*"
Journal of School Psychology 17(1): 87–88.

Zubizarreta, John. 1995. "Using Teaching Portfolio Strategies to

Improve Course Instruction." In *Improving College Teaching,* edited by Peter Seldin. Bolton, Mass.: Anker Publishing.

INDEX

assimilating learners, 69

    instructors expected to be disseminators of information, 71

Association of American Colleges

    need for better preparation of college teachers, 4

Astin, Alexander W., 11, 24

Awareness in Five-Step Process for Improving Teaching, 20

B

Ball State University, 47, 55

basic instructional skills program, 52-53

Bloom's Taxonomy (1956), 75, 59

    classifies educational objectives into six separate categories, 75

        sample questions, 91

Bok's (1986) recommendations for improving university learning

    applies to Diamond (1989) model, 80

Bowen, Howard, 11

Boyd, William, 11

Boyer, Carol M., 11

British Columbia Ministry of Education, 51, 54

C

Carnegie-Mellon University Doctor of Arts degree, 4

CATS. See classroom assessment techniques

Center for Community College Education, ix-x

Center for Improving Teaching and Learning, 7

    national resource for information on instructional practice, 45

Center for the Improvement of Teaching and Learning

    spread of the concept of, 46-47

Centers for Improving Teaching, 45-47

change theory principles

    Great Teachers Seminar based upon, 36

Chickering, Arthur W. and Zelda F. Gamson

    provided the substance for process of generating feedback, 11

    See also Seven Principles for Good Practice in Education wide impact of work of, 15

CIAS. See Cognitive Interaction Analysis System

City Colleges of Chicago, 45

Classification Systems

    Sample Questions Using, 91

Classroom Assessment model, 7, 23-30

    access to, 26

    advantages of, 29

Curriculum Pedagogy Assessment theory, 81

electronic organizers, 65

Episode of Teaching Growth, 32-33

ERIC Clearinghouse on Higher Education, 49

essential aspect of the role of faculty
    perpetual instructional development, 86

Evaluation
        data, 33-34
        in Five-Step Process for Improving Teaching, 21

The Experiential Learning Cycle, 68-69

Excel Inc. provides 4MAT" training, 70, 89

Experiential Learning and 4MAT", 68-71

expert software systems use, 81

external events that could influence students' learning, 77

Exxon Education Foundation, 39

F

Facilitator Skills Workshop, 53

faculty behavior in the classroom
        four combinations or clusters that depict, 73

Faculty-Driven Improvement, 83-84

faculty interventions, 71

Faculty Inventory of Good Practice, 11-15
    designed for instructors who wish to improve their
    teaching, 13
    recognized as a helpful diagnostic tool, 15
    still available from Seven Principles Resource Center, 15

feedback
    faculty deprived of opportunity to consider the use and value of,
        2
    session, 52

Feldman and Newcomb (1969), 24

Fife, Jonathan D.
    activities that will result in teaching quality improvement, ix-x

Five-Step Process for Improving Teaching, 19-23
    Awareness in, 20
    designed for the exclusive use of the faculty members, 20
    Evaluation in, 21
    Implementation of plan in, 21
    influence on improvement of, 22-23
    Information retrieval in, 21
    plan for gathering feedback considered Òexemplary,Ó 22-23
    selection of alternatives in, 21
    Weimer (1990) supported with an extensive research base, 22

Four-Phase Feedback, 32
4MAT", 70-72
　　　praise of, 72
　　　for information about, 89
　　　implemented by U.S. state staff developers and, 71-72
　　　training program, 8

G

Gaff, Jerry, 11

Gagn≥, Robert M.　See also　Instructional Event Design
　　　examination of events that could influence students'
　　　learning, 77
　　　value of conceptual model of, 79

Gardner, Howard.　See also　multiple intelligences and teaching
　　　praise of model, 67
　　　theory, 66

Garrison, Roger
　　experimental faculty development seminar in Maine of, 35

gathering questions
　　in Dantonio's (1990) questioning processes, 76

generalization learning, 60-62
　　　direct instruction, 60-61
　　　discovery strategy, 62-63
　　　model generalization, 60-61
　　　objective generalization category identification, 61

George Washington University, 49

Ògoal ranking and matchingÓ technique, 27-28

Gottshall, David
　　Illinois Great Teachers Seminar developed by, 35

Grasha, Anthony F. model.　See also　teaching styles
　　　　four combinations for faculty behavior in the classroom, 73
　　　　integration of teaching and learning styles, 8
　　　　evaluation of, 74
　　　　linking learning style insight to teaching applications, 72
　　　　provides faculty tool to improve teaching and learning, 74

Great Teachers Seminar, 7, 35-39
　　　　based upon change theory principles, 36
　　　　chief means for disseminating the model, 39
　　　　focus entire experience on pragmatic and supportive
　　　　efforts, 37
　　　　four basic presumptions, 36
　　　　necessary characteristics of, 36-38
　　　　operative word is ÒsharingÓ in, 37

grid of effective instruction, 18

GTS. See Great Teachers Seminar

Òguided practice,Ó 78

guides available for faculty development of questioning skills, 76

H

Halsted, Henry, 11

Harvard University, 47

Hierarchies as technique for organizing information, 62

Hierarchy of Models for improving college teaching, 64

higher education's impact on students syntheses of research, 24

Hughes, Billie

    introduced author to models for improving college teaching, xi

human memory theory and its application to learning, 62

I

Illinois Great Teachers Seminar developed by David Gottshall, 35

individuality of learning process

    key to improving learning for all students is recognition of, 2

information processing utility, 65

Innovation Absracts, 47, 48

    for information about, 89

    circulation figures for, 50

Innovative Higher Education, 47

Institutional support for experimentation to enhance learning, 84

Institutions' Implementation of the Models, 84-85

institutions must provide faculty opportunities to assess and

        develop teaching skills, ix

instructional design skills lesson, 52

Instructional Event Design, 8, 77-79. See also Gagn≥, Robert M.

Instructional Planning Models, 8, 77-81

instructional questions should transcend probes of memory, 75

instructional skills dissemination, 54

Instructional Skills Workshop, 7, 51-54

        conducted on 50 American campuses, 54

        developed for the British Columbia Ministry of Education,

        51

Integrating Teaching and Learning Styles, 72-74

integration of teaching and learning styles of Grasha, 8

intellectual excitement, instructor who elicits,16

Intelligent learning, 67-68

Òinternal processÓ as learning, 77

interpersonal rapport, instructor who elicits, 17

interpreting questions

in Dantonio's (1990) questioning processes, 76

intersecting dimensions, 17-18

inventories as contributors to good practice, 13-14

Iowa Great Teachers Workshop at Lake Okoboji, 35

ISW. See Instructional Skills Workshop

J

James Rhem and Associates, 49

Johnson Foundation, 11

   faculty inventory distributed by, 15

   republished Seven Principles, 14

Journal on Excellence in College Teaching, 47

judgment in Bloom's taxonomy, 75

K

Katz, Joseph, 11

key elements in each lesson, 52

key to improving learning for all students is recognition of

   individuality of learning process, 2

knowledge in Bloom's taxonomy, 75

knowledge of content

   as defining characteristic of pedagogical accomplishment, 3

knowledge types that are the most basic stages of learning, 59

Kolb, David A.

      concepts, 68

      Dimensions of Learning, 8

      Learning Cycle, 69

      Learning Styles Inventory, 69

Kolb's (1984) model, 68-69

      incorporated in 4MAT", 70

      Svinicki & Dixon (1987) classroom techniques for each phase,
      70

L

Lazear (1991) model on multiple intelligences

      for faculty using in three ways, 66

      for applying multiple intelligences to teaching, 8

learners, need to take account of differences in teaching, 68

learning

      as an Òinternal processÓ (Gagn≥ 1965, 1970), 77

      focus of educational institutions should shift from teaching
      to, 1

minilesson, 52

Òminute paperÓ CAT that seems to have achieved the widest use, 27

model

applying to improve College Teaching, 83

for designing entire curricula as well as individual courses, 79

for faculty to incorporate multiple intelligences, 66

generalization in Generalization learning, 60-61

linking insight gained from examining learning styles to applications for teaching, 72

use of, 8-9

multifaceted approach for gathering feedback from students, 23

multiple intelligences and teaching, 65-68. See also Howard Gardner

model for faculty to incorporate in three ways, 66

need to design teaching methods with dominant one in mind, 67

model of Lazear applied to teaching, 8

Òmultiplier effect,Ó 45

N

National Center for Education Statistics (1994), 15

National Center for Research

on Post secondary Teaching, Learning, and Assessment, 5

National Endowment for the Humanities, 39

National Institute for Staff and Organizational Development, 5

National Teaching and Learning Forum, 47, 49

circulation figures for, 50

information about, 89

newsletters for improving college teaching circulation, 50

NISOD. See National Institute for Staff & Organizational Development

O

objective generalization category in Generalization learning, 61

Ohio State University, 43, 47

organizing questions

in Dantonio's (1990) questioning processes, 76

P

Pace, C. Robert, 11, 24

Pacific Northwest Great Teachers Seminar, 35

passive learners
    instructional practices that force students to remain, 3
passive lecture technique, frequent criticisms of, 12
Peaks model, 81
peer teaching, 43
perpetual instructional development
    essential aspect of the role of faculty, 86
PERT. See program evaluation and review technique
Peterson, Marvin W., 11
positive student behavior
    quality circles as a powerful motivating incentive for, 32
preparation of many college and university faculty for teaching
    shortchanged in at least four ways, 2
Preparation of trainers, 53
procedural memory, 58
Professional and Organizational Development Network in Higher
        Education, 4-5, 47
program evaluation and review technique
        chart, 63
        Diagram example, 65
        similar to Diamond (1989) model, 79
Publications, as a means of improving teaching and learning, 47-50

Q
quality circles, 31-32
quality of teaching on college campuses
    activities that will result in a significant improvement in, ix-x
questioning skills
    guides available for faculty members' development of, 76
Questionnaire for Planing Classroom Assessment, 26

R
Reading
        as common activity by which faculty gather new ideas, 47
        List for College Teaching, 87-88
        ÒratingÓ technique, 28
Recall learning, 59-60
        elaboration technique of, 60
        rehearsal technique of, 60
        reconfiguring great amounts of data technique of, 60
        rehearsal technique of, 60
Òrepeatable categories,Ó 64
Resource List, 89

Since 1983, the Association for the Study of Higher Educa-tion (ASHE) and the Educational Resources Information Center (ERIC) Clearinghouse on Higher Education, a spon-sored project of the Graduate School of Education and Human Development at The George Washington University, have cosponsored the ASHE-ERIC Higher Education Report series. The 1995 series is the twenty-fourth overall and the seventh to be published by the Graduate School of Educa-tion and Human Development at The George Washington University.

Each monograph is the definitive analysis of a tough higher education problem, based on thorough research of pertinent literature and institutional experiences. Topics are identified by a national survey. Noted practitioners and scholars are then commissioned to write the reports, with experts providing critical reviews of each manuscript before publication.

Eight monographs (10 before 1985) in the ASHE-ERIC Higher Education Report series are published each year and are available on individual and subscription bases. To order, use the order form on the last page of this book.

Qualified persons interested in writing a monograph for the ASHE-ERIC Higher Education Report series are invited to submit a proposal to the National Advisory Board. As the preeminent literature review and issue analysis series in higher education, the Higher Education Reports are guaran-teed wide dissemination and national exposure for accepted candidates. Execution of a monograph requires at least a minimal familiarity with the ERIC database, including *Resources in Education* and the current *Index to Journals in Education*. The objective of these reports is to bridge con-ventional wisdom with practical research. Prospective authors are strongly encouraged to call Dr. Fife at 800-773-3742.

For further information, write to
    ASHE-ERIC Higher Education Reports
    The George Washington University
    One Dupont Circle, Suite 630
    Washington, DC 20036
Or phone (202) 296-2597; toll free: 800-773-ERIC.

Write or call for a complete catalog.

ADVISORY BOARD

James Earl Davis
University of Delaware at Newark

Susan Frost
Emory University

Mildred Garcia
Montclair State College

James Hearn
University of Georgia

Bruce Anthony Jones
University of Pittsburgh

L. Jackson Newell
Deep Springs College

Carolyn Thompson
State University of New York–Buffalo

Diane E. Morrison
Centre for Curriculum and Professional Development

L. Jackson Newell
University of Utah

Steven G. Olswang
University of Washington

Sherry Sayles-Folks
Eastern Michigan University

Karl Schilling
Miami University

Charles Schroeder
University of Missouri

Lawrence A. Sherr
University of Kansas

Marilla D. Svinicki
University of Texas at Austin

David Sweet
OERI, U.S. Department of Education

Kathe Taylor
State of Washington Higher Education Coordinating Board

Donald H. Wulff
University of Washington

Manta Yorke
Liverpool John Moores University

REVIEW PANEL

Charles Adams
University of Massachusetts–Amherst

Louis Albert
American Association for Higher Education

Richard Alfred
University of Michigan

Henry Lee Allen
University of Rochester

Philip G. Altbach
Boston College

Marilyn J. Amey
University of Kansas

Kristine L. Anderson
Florida Atlantic University

Karen D. Arnold
Boston College

Robert J. Barak
Iowa State Board of Regents

Alan Bayer
Virginia Polytechnic Institute and State University

John P. Bean
Indiana University–Bloomington

John M. Braxton
Peabody College, Vanderbilt University

Ellen M. Brier
Tennessee State University

Barbara E. Brittingham
The University of Rhode Island

Dennis Brown
University of Kansas

Peter McE. Buchanan
Council for Advancement and Support of Education

Patricia Carter
University of Michigan

John A. Centra
Syracuse University

Arthur W. Chickering
George Mason University

Darrel A. Clowes
Virginia Polytechnic Institute and State University

Cynthia S. Dickens
Mississippi State University

Deborah M. DiCroce
Piedmont Virginia Community College

Sarah M. Dinham
University of Arizona

Kenneth A. Feldman
State University of New York–Stony Brook

Dorothy E. Finnegan
The College of William & Mary

Mildred Garcia
Montclair State College

Rodolfo Z. Garcia
Commission on Institutions of Higher Education

Kenneth C. Green
University of Southern California

James Hearn
University of Georgia

Edward R. Hines
Illinois State University

Deborah Hunter
University of Vermont

Philo Hutcheson
Georgia State University

Bruce Anthony Jones
University of Pittsburgh

Elizabeth A. Jones
The Pennsylvania State University

Kathryn Kretschmer
University of Kansas

Marsha V. Krotseng
State College and University Systems of West Virginia

George D. Kuh
Indiana University–Bloomington

Daniel T. Layzell
University of Wisconsin System

Patrick G. Love
Kent State University

Cheryl D. Lovell
State Higher Education Executive Officers

Meredith Jane Ludwig
American Association of State Colleges and Universities

Dewayne Matthews
Western Interstate Commission for Higher Education

Mantha V. Mehallis
Florida Atlantic University

Toby Milton
Essex Community College

James R. Mingle
State Higher Education Executive Officers

John A. Muffo
Virginia Polytechnic Institute and State University

L. Jackson Newell
Deep Springs College

James C. Palmer
Illinois State University

Robert A. Rhoads
The Pennsylvania State University

G. Jeremiah Ryan
Harford Community College

Mary Ann Danowitz Sagaria
The Ohio State University

Daryl G. Smith
The Claremont Graduate School

William G. Tierney
University of Southern California

Susan B. Twombly
University of Kansas

Robert A. Walhaus
University of Illinois–Chicago

Harold Wechsler
University of Rochester

Elizabeth J. Whitt
University of Illinois–Chicago

Michael J. Worth
The George Washington University

RECENT TITLES

1995 ASHE-ERIC Higher Education Reports

1. Tenure, Promotion, and Reappointment: Legal and Administrative Implications
   Benjamin Baez and John A. Centra

2. Taking Teaching Seriously: Meeting the Challenge of Instructional Improvement
   Michael B. Paulsen and Kenneth A. Feldman

3. Empowering the Faculty: Mentoring Redirected and Renewed
   Gaye Luna and Deborah L. Cullen

4. Enhancing Student Learning: Intellectual, Social, and Emotional Integration
   Anne Goodsell Love and Patrick G. Love

5. Benchmarking in Higher Education: Adapting Best Practices to Improve Quality
   Jeffrey W. Alstete

1994 ASHE-ERIC Higher Education Reports

1. The Advisory Committee Advantage: Creating an Effective Strategy for Programmatic Improvement
   Lee Teitel

2. Collaborative Peer Review: The Role of Faculty in Improving College Teaching
   Larry Keig and Michael D. Waggoner

3. Prices, Productivity, and Investment: Assessing Financial Strategies in Higher Education
   Edward P. St. John

4. The Development Officer in Higher Education: Toward an Understanding of the Role
   Michael J. Worth and James W. Asp II

5. The Promises and Pitfalls of Performance Indicators in Higher Education
   Gerald Gaither, Brian P. Nedwek, and John E. Neal

6. A New Alliance: Continuous Quality and Classroom Effectiveness
   Mimi Wolverton

7. Redesigning Higher Education: Producing Dramatic Gains in Student Learning
   Lion F. Gardiner

8. Student Learning outside the Classroom: Transcending Artificial Boundaries
   George D. Kuh, Katie Branch Douglas, Jon P. Lund, and Jackie Ramin-Gyurnek

---

1993 ASHE-ERIC Higher Education Reports

1. The Department Chair: New Roles, Responsibilities, and Challenges
   Alan T. Seagren, John W. Creswell, and Daniel W. Wheeler

2. Sexual Harassment in Higher Education: From Conflict to Community
   Robert O. Riggs, Patricia H. Murrell, and Joann C. Cutting

3. Chicanos in Higher Education: Issues and Dilemmas for the 21st Century
   Adalberto Aguirre, Jr., and Ruben O. Martinez

4. Academic Freedom in American Higher Education: Rights, Responsibilities, and Limitations
   Robert K. Poch

5. Making Sense of the Dollars: The Costs and Uses of Faculty Compensation
   Kathryn M. Moore and Marilyn J. Amey

6. Enhancing Promotion, Tenure, and Beyond: Faculty Socialization as a Cultural Process
   William C. Tierney and Robert A. Rhoads

7. New Perspectives for Student Affairs Professionals: Evolving Realities, Responsibilities, and Roles
   Peter H. Garland and Thomas W. Grace

8. Turning Teaching into Learning: The Role of Student Responsibility in the Collegiate Experience
   Todd M. Davis and Patricia Hillman Murrell

1992 ASHE-ERIC Higher Education Reports

1. The Leadership Compass: Values and Ethics in Higher Education
   John R. Wilcox and Susan L. Ebbs

2. Preparing for a Global Community: Achieving an International Perspective in Higher Education
   Sarah M. Pickert

3. Quality: Transforming Postsecondary Education
   Ellen Earle Chaffee and Lawrence A. Sherr

4. Faculty Job Satisfaction: Women and Minorities in Peril
   Martha Wingard Tack and Carol Logan Patitu

5. Reconciling Rights and Responsibilities of Colleges and Students: Offensive Speech, Assembly, Drug Testing, and Safety
   Annette Gibbs

6. Creating Distinctiveness: Lessons from Uncommon Colleges and Universities
   Barbara K. Townsend, L. Jackson Newell, and Michael D. Wiese

7. Instituting Enduring Innovations: Achieving Continuity of Change in Higher Education
   Barbara K. Curry

8. Crossing Pedagogical Oceans: International Teaching Assistants in U.S. Undergraduate Education
   Rosslyn M. Smith, Patricia Byrd, Gayle L. Nelson, Ralph Pat Barrett, and Janet C. Constantinides

1991 ASHE-ERIC Higher Education Reports

1. Active Learning: Creating Excitement in the Classroom
   Charles C. Bonwell and James A. Eison

2. Realizing Gender Equality in Higher Education: The Need to Integrate Work/Family Issues
   Nancy Hensel

3. Academic Advising for Student Success: A System of Shared Responsibility
   Susan H. Frost

4. Cooperative Learning: Increasing College Faculty Instructional Productivity
   David W. Johnson, Roger T. Johnson, and Karl A. Smith

5. High School–College Partnerships: Conceptual Models, Programs, and Issues
   Arthur Richard Greenberg

6. Meeting the Mandate: Renewing the College and Departmental Curriculum
   William Toombs and William Tierney

7. Faculty Collaboration: Enhancing the Quality of Scholarship and Teaching
   Ann E. Austin and Roger G. Baldwin

8. Strategies and Consequences: Managing the Costs in Higher Education
   John S. Waggaman

ORDER FORM

Quantity   **Amount**

_____ Please begin my subscription to the 1996 *ASHE-ERIC Higher Education Reports (Volume 25)* at $98.00, 31% off the cover price, starting with Report 1, 1995. Includes shipping. _____

_____ Please send a complete set of the 1995 *ASHE-ERIC Higher Education Reports* at $98.00, 31% off the cover price. Please add shipping charge below. _____

Individual reports are available at the following prices:
1993, 1994, and 1995, $18.00; 1988–1992, $17.00; 1980–1987, $15.00

SHIPPING CHARGES
For orders of more than 50 books, please call for shipping information.

	1st three books	*Ea. addl. book*
U.S., 48 Contiguous States		
Ground:	$3.75	$0.15
2nd Day*:	8.25	1.10
Next Day*:	18.00	1.60
Alaska & Hawaii (2nd Day Only)*:	13.25	1.40

U.S. Territories and Foreign Countries: Please call for shipping information.
*Order will be shipped within 24 hours of request.
All prices shown on this form are subject to change.

PLEASE SEND ME THE FOLLOWING REPORTS:

Quantity	Report No.	Year	Title	Amount

Please check one of the following:
☐ Check enclosed, payable to GWU-ERIC.
☐ Purchase order attached.
☐ Charge my credit card indicated below:
  ☐ Visa   ☐ MasterCard

Subtotal: _____

Shipping: _____

Total Due: _____

Expiration Date_____

Name_____

Title_____

Institution _____

Address_____

City _____ State _____ Zip_____

Phone _____ Fax _____ Telex_____

Signature _____ Date_____

SEND ALL ORDERS TO: ASHE-ERIC Higher Education Reports
The George Washington University
One Dupont Cir., Ste. 630, Washington, DC 20036-1183
Phone: (202) 296-2597 • Toll-free: 800-773-ERIC